D1298272

The Core Meaning

Chris Raper

Catherine –

May God bless you always.

C. B. Raper

To God:

I am humbled in your presence. Thank you for the challenges you have put in my path and the determination you placed in my heart. I know now that without my relationship with you, I am nothing.

To my wife:

The day I said, "I do," my life was finally complete and God has given me everything a man could ask for. Your support gives me the drive to continue following my dreams. I look forward to our continued journey together. God has great things in store for us. I love you.

To my daughter:

I am so proud of you. You are the sweetest, loving and most caring person. Your ability to adapt to situations is simply amazing. You are truly my inspiration and I love you.

To my family and friends:

You have all played a part in this journey. Life's experiences are what truly give us passion and drive. If it were not for each of you, I would be a different person. Thank you for each time our paths have crossed and for the positive imprints left by each intersection.

Table of Contents

Preface

The challenges we experience in life provide us with the greatest opportunity to reflect on God's grace. Yet most of the time we are so caught up in the problems and ourselves that we can't seem to figure out how to get past them. I spent a fair amount of time there over the past ten years. This decade has been full of great achievements and severe disappointments. Each of these places, even as polar as they seem, have given me the strength to prosper and make it through. These experiences have made me a much better Christian, husband, father, son, brother, and friend. The primary objective of this devotional is to give hope and a format of reflection for those who are going through life's challenges or have made it through a tough time, yet can't seem to forgive the person (or persons) who caused the pain. (Hint: That's all of us.)

These writings were completed at various times through the years and never really came together until Easter of 2010. As I mentioned to my wife over and over and over again, I was going to write a book. She heard what I said, but didn't see me do anything. Primarily because all I did was talk. I had these writings, but did not know what to do with them, other than the fact that I wanted to write a book. She gave me a challenge for Lent in 2010 to begin writing this book, if that was truly what I wanted to do. That was the push I needed. I am pretty sure that without her challenge, this book would still be on sheets of paper somewhere around my desk.

I offer you this history, because this process is very similar to how we live our lives. We know we want something, but either we don't think we can do it or someone tells us that we are not smart enough to do it, etc. We should be listening to the one person who has all the answers—God. He will put things and people in our lives to help shape and guide us, yet we must cultivate our relationship with him in order to fully see these opportunities. We must forgive as he forgives. We must love as he loves. We must believe in ourselves as much as he believes in us. A purpose is within each of us to fulfill during our limited lifespan. Be sure not to miss it while caught up in life's more unimportant activities.

There are too many people to personally thank each for their support and feedback. All of you, along with these writings, have allowed this book to happen and therefore give hope to someone who needs a hand. God truly put the right people in my path—I just opened my eyes.

C.B. Raper

Foreword and Introduction

This book has been in my heart for a very long time. Many versions have been considered, but now I have begun. This journey started over a decade ago as things changed in my life and I tried to understand their purposes. Those life changes included a divorce, my father's death and the birth of my daughter. Each of these has shaped my life in a very positive manner. Yet I was still challenged by one thing: my faith. It was weak. Church seemed to only be a meeting each week, not a relationship with Jesus Christ.

How that challenge played out is a great story and focuses how I want my legacy to read: *it was for someone else*. My daughter was young when it hit me that I might not be able to answer the foundational questions that she would inevitably ask about our religion and God. I immediately got the feeling that "because I said so" would be my easy way out of the situation. That thought process started the most amazing journey—one that I am still enjoying. I began taking church more seriously and started to ask a lot of questions. Not all of the answers were what I expected or wanted to hear. For example, we are supposed to forgive others as God forgave us. But wait a minute—we were hurt by these people. All of us have been there and have struggled with that situation. Some have felt how great it is to truly forgive and see the change it makes in everyone's life.

My life did not change overnight after I decided to take my faith more seriously. If it had, this book never would have even been considered. Quite the opposite—I had three of the most painful years of my life that shook my foundation to the core. I struggled for years with how God could allow these things to happen in my life. Surely I had no part in creating any of this. (Sound familiar?)

Hebrews 12:4–8

> *In your struggle against sin, you have not yet resisted to the point of shedding your blood. And you have forgotten that word of encouragement that addresses you as sons: "My son, do not make light of the Lord's discipline, and do not lose heart when he rebukes you, because the*

Lord disciplines those he loves, and he punishes everyone he accepts as a son." Endure hardship as discipline; God is treating you as sons. For what son is not disciplined by his father? If you are not disciplined (and everyone undergoes discipline), then you are illegitimate children and not true sons.

I learned during these difficult times that when you think there is no one else to support you and no money to make you temporally feel better, God helps you find the real purpose of life. After being at nearly rock bottom a couple of times, my faith grew stronger and my drive gained more clarity. I was a father and I needed to educate myself so that my daughter would have the best opportunities in this world.

I will get to the world part of this journey in a moment, but let me share with you how a relatively "normal" guy ends up writing inspirational faith-based poetry and still feels macho (that is what it's all about, right?). Be strong, don't cry, be a man—just kidding. Cry with your family one time and then say emotions are not the language of God. First of all, you have to understand it is never about me. At least, it should not be. I am definitely not perfect and I am truly broken in God's presence.

These writings began during a golf tournament in which I was invited to play by a great friend, who is now my spiritual confidant and mentor. The tournament was in memory of a gentleman who had recently passed away, so before the tournament began, there was a prayer in the clubhouse. My first thought was, *Awkward!* I pondered the thought of God and golf in public and said to myself, *Whatever happened to birdies and beers?* My thoughts continued, *I bet they will do just fine with only three players.* But then it began. The prayer leader talked about how this man would have connected God and golf. He said, "Pick a target, line up, and follow through." My life changed that day in the clubhouse. I already knew the "target." It was God. Now I needed to do something.

As life goes, we get busy and great intentions seem to fall by the wayside. Yet this feeling would not go away. One night out of nowhere, I wrote my first poem, entitled "The Who" (in this book re-titled "Renew"). From that point forward, everything was put in a greater perspective and my "religion" or "faith" or whatever it was at the time, transformed into an amazing relationship with Jesus Christ. A friend asked me once if I had this kind of personal relationship. Another "awkward" moment followed because I was not ready with an honest answer. I think anyone who knows me realizes the answer to that question. It took a while but—yes!

Okay, now back to the world comment I made earlier. It seems that we as people have steered into a materialistic "I" lifestyle that clearly has its pitfalls. Watch your local or world news station for proof of that. Before I continue, let me assure you that there was a time I could not keep up with the Joneses fast enough. I have paid dearly for that chase. I feel we have lost touch with our family values, our perspective on need, the importance of faith and our true purpose in life. As my writing continued and God's purposes for me came together, it was clear what I needed to do. In a world of quick fixes, which require another quick fix shortly thereafter, I wanted to create an inward journey for individuals to reflect on their lives and find their "core meaning."

This book is Volume I of a planned four-volume devotional series dedicated to help facilitate a personal journey, through which you may find your purpose from God. You may even find God for the first time, which will change your life. Included in Volume I are sixteen devotions. Each devotion consists of a text segment, associated scripture, my personal reflections and a five-day study guide. I surely can't say I had God sitting with me when I wrote all of these; however, I sit with him every day now and I am so much better off for that.

So how does the "normal guy" feel about writing poetry? He has seen the great things God can do. If a few more people (men or women) can feel what I feel, then I think poetry rocks. Have a conversation with your child, your friend, or your mate about how you truly feel deep inside your heart and watch the magic happen. If you don't believe me—try it. The core of anything has to be strong to survive and overcome. Let's do our part.

I recommend dedicating a week to each devotional. The associated scriptures are several verses that tie in biblical meaning and context of the poem for me. I realized, as a part of putting this book together, that a great benefit of this format is exposure to God's word and the excitement that can bring. While there are only three verses provided for each weekly devotional, my hope is that you gain more understanding by following the 5-day study format. Each writing clearly has a specific meaning to me. I expect you will connect to each writing in your own way. That is because we are all unique. The objective is to gain a deeper perspective of your journey. I am by no means a biblical scholar, so please do not consider my thoughts as a perfect translation of God's word. However, my perspective is from what I feel he was speaking to me through these verses and how they transformed my life.

I can only hope this book allows me to help one person in a tough spot or that one person takes their life to a new level. If this is helpful to you, get a copy for a friend and watch God come on the scene of their life. If you see it happen, please visit www.thecoremeaning.com and share the story.

Enjoy your journey and may God's purposes for your life be revealed or grasped more firmly.

Purpose

We wake each day with great ideas of how to achieve it
Many hours of tears and excitement surround the thought
Yet each step towards the realization creates more questions
We all know that something bigger lies ahead—purpose;

Culture drives us to think the end results must be big
Turning of a key is a simple thing, but gives us peace of mind
Blowing a bubble makes a child laugh out loud and takes only effort
Remember, big may be the result, impactful is your purpose;

It will not be easy, consider the path Jesus took for our salvation
There were no beds of roses, only pain and suffering for the greater good
You may never see your ultimate impacts, yet others will be changed forever
A pebble dropped in a pond never sees what the last ripple does—purpose;

Knowing that your life is impacting another helps solidify each day
Wishing you had done something yesterday is a waste of today
Remember you may be a step in someone else's journey at any moment—be ready
Live in the moment, be present and have true meaning and purpose;

A rocking chair in perfect view of the sunset is where you rest
Your life has given you many options and choices for greatness as God defines it
As the sun meets the ocean in the horizon, its daily purpose is met
The tear riding your cheek—is it sadness or the culmination of a fulfilled purpose?

Don't let people say, "I know he wanted to ..."

Purpose—Opening Personal Reflection

Purpose is something we all seem to struggle with at different points in our lives. One day, we feel strongly that following a certain path is the right thing to do; however, we don't get the fulfillment we expected in return. As we look at others, we may feel deficient because they seem so focused and we are still searching. Our true purpose is not found in others, but placed on our hearts by our Savior Jesus Christ. Remember this is about God and not you, so don't feel left out. That pebble in the pond may have saved the life of one of God's tiny creatures, but the pebble never knows that fact.

My purpose only came to me in my mid-thirties, via a gift of writing and a deeper meaning of God's word. Your purpose in life may be something off the wall, like mine, or clear and connected to your current life's activities. Either way, be sure to stay present and watch attentively for what God has put in your life.

Take the time this week to reflect on all the things you do in life and always ensure that you ask God for guidance each step of the way. His ways are amazing and so too are you when connected with his desires.

Associated Scripture Verses

2 Timothy 1:9
... who has saved us and called us to a holy life—not because of anything we have done but because of his own purpose and grace. This grace was given us in Christ Jesus before the beginning of time ...

Romans 8:28
And we know that in all things God works for the good of those who love him, who have been called according to his purpose.

2 Corinthians 5:5
Now it is God who has made us for this very purpose and has given us the Spirit as a deposit, guaranteeing what is to come.

Day 1

Read: Purpose, Associated Scripture Verses and Opening Personal
Reflection —

Activity: Take time to consider what purposes God may have placed in
your life. Write down the thoughts that come to mind. They will
be used later in the week.

Purpose Thoughts:

_____

_____

_____

_____

Prayer: Dear Lord, please give me clarity regarding the purposes you have
for my life. Allow me to connect the events in my life that lead me
to those purposes. Magnify the gifts you have given me, so that I
may put them to full use. Open my mind and heart this week as I
search for unique purposes you have for me. In the name of Jesus
Christ, I pray. Amen.

Day 2

Read: 2 Timothy 1

Review: Purpose Thoughts from Day 1

Activity: As you reflect on the scripture reading of Paul's Second Letter to
Timothy, focus on three key themes: Thankfulness (1:3-7), Courage
(1:8-12) and Faithfulness (1:13-18). How do these themes integrate
into your purpose thoughts? Or do they? Spend time writing down

your understanding from each section and how each topic relates to what you think God's purpose may be in your life.

Thankfulness

_____

_____

_____

_____

Courage

_____

_____

_____

_____

Faithfulness

_____

_____

_____

_____

Prayer: Dear Lord, give me the Thankfulness, Courage and Faithfulness today to gain additional clarity of my purpose. Allow me to gain more understanding in your time and in your way. Open my mind to things that might seem out of place or new interests that I have not had before. Also create in me an aware mind, so that I may think more clearly. In the name of Jesus Christ, I pray. Amen.

Day 3

Read: Romans 8.

Review: Theme Understandings from Day 2

Activity: Focus on four Key Areas from Romans: Living through the Spirit (8:1-11), Standard of Living (8:12-17), Living with Hope (8:18-30), and Living with Confidence (8:31-39). Provide an impact statement (i.e. how does it impact your purpose) for each key area.

Living through the Spirit

_____

_____

_____

_____

Standard of Living

_____

_____

_____

_____

Living with Hope

_____

_____

_____

_____

Living with Confidence

_____

_____

_____

_____

Prayer: Dear Lord, guide me through life's challenges with purpose, protect me from being too "me" centered and allow me to help others first. Give me the heart of a servant leader, where I may grow only when I help others grow. I ask you for prosperity in the image of God. Show me the way to a Spirit Life and help me to focus my attention and center my life in that place. In the name of Jesus Christ, I pray. Amen.

Day 4

Read: 2 Corinthians 5

Review: Impact Statements from Day 3

Activity: Answer the following questions:

As it relates to Christianity, what do you take away as the main point of Chapter 5?

_____

_____

_____

_____

Do the things you do or have done so far in your life make you fear the judgment seat?

_____

_____

_____

_____

How does God's offer of reconciliation help you with the question above?

_____

_____

_____

_____

Prayer: Dear Lord, give me guidance to open questions in my heart. Let the answers to these questions give me peace and purpose. Provide me a path to helping others, as your Son so helped us by dying on the cross for our sins and returning to watch over us for eternity. In the name of Jesus Christ, I pray. Amen.

Day 5

Read: Purpose

Reflect: Your notes from each of the exercises this week.

Activity: Now that you see it is not about you, but God—How does this change the definition of purpose you had before this week started? How has the purpose you wrote on Day 1 this week changed or become clearer?

_____

_____

_____

_____

Purpose—Closing Personal Reflections

We must give up our lives in order to truly live. God will never let us be naked or without when we have given our lives to him. God prepares us each day for something and we will see it when we fully allow him into our lives. At that point, we live by faith and not sight. The Spirit guides us through our purposes. We just need to trust and accept them. Our goal is to please Christ in our actions.

God offers reconciliation for the paths we have taken in life. The fact that we have sinned does not mean we are not worthy—we are just normal. We realize Christ died for us and gives us hope. We now live through him and for his purposes. This provides a new life through Christ. The only path for this type of transformation is through him. Our sins are not held against us, so become an ambassador and spread his word. By following our purposes, we glorify Christ. If we are pre-destined for a purpose, then we must stop fighting so hard against it. Give in to God's greatness. He sent his only Son to take our sin away and for us to live by the Spirit, which gives us life, so we can let our bodies die to sin.

If Jesus' death was a sacrifice to take all our sins away ...
And sin brings death to the mortal body ...
Then we are alive through Christ.
There has to be something giving you life and purpose.

That is the Holy Spirit.
Now, if you are willing to go that far—is it really too much to say we have purpose in us born
from God?

If not, welcome to Romans 8:30: *And those he predestined, he also called; those he called,
he also justified; those he justified, he also glorified.*

Go for it! I did!

Transform

The places where we are and we want to be, seem so polar
Fulfillment in each area creates confusion that freezes movement
We know that one of these places is selfish in nature
Your mind knows change is necessary, but no action seems to—transform;

Constant struggle exists in the journey away from this revered place
Attempts in the past have been for a reason—just not the right one
Others, not you, felt you spent too much time there
Real change can't happen by or for others—only you—transform;

Your optimal place in God's world is located within your heart
The roller coaster ride through your body to that place is long and dark
To achieve your purpose in life, that journey must be shortened
The impurities you place in your body are slowing your trip—transform;

Keeping a close connection to your destination is paramount
There may be a divine change in direction—be present for those signs
Your roadblocks are simply yield signs of fear and confusion
Take the highway your Creator built for you—he is waiting—transform;

Life provides you with many choices and places to travel
Each one of them has a destination with personal exits along the way
Limited exits off the highway of purpose may lead you to great realizations
You already have the materials, and he awaits your surrender—transform.

Associated Scripture Verses

Philippians 3:21
... who, by the power that enables him to bring everything under his control, will transform our lowly bodies so that they will be like his glorious body.

Romans 12:2
Do not conform any longer to the pattern of this world, but be transformed by the renewing of your mind. Then you will be able to test and approve what God's will is—his good, pleasing and perfect will.

2 Corinthians 3:18
And we, who with unveiled faces all reflect the Lord's glory, are being transformed into his likeness with ever-increasing glory, which comes from the Lord, who is the Spirit.

Transform—Opening Personal Reflection

Change can scare even the most grounded person in this world. We all struggle with things in our lives that seem a bit uncontrollable. Actions we take that make us happy for a short period may be taking big chunks of time off the end. A very close friend of mine inspired this writing and has struggled with some of the actions in her life. The struggle with alcohol was not disastrous, yet it impacted her family and work in a negative way. Realizing this impact is what changed her actions. Her focus is now regained. Drinking is not taboo, but understanding the impact of it is very clear. Seems the Bible is always right! It is not wrong to drink alcohol, but we should make sure we understand moderation.

As you think of how transformation can work in your life, I ask you to think of others and not assume you have to do it alone. In community with others, we raise the bar higher than we could as only one single piece of the solution. Your actions may have more impact on others than on yourself. If you experience that growth, then you have experienced what it truly feels like to be a servant leader. May God be with you always, particularly this week as you begin to take a transformational look inside.

Day 1

Read: Transform, Associated Scripture Verses and Opening Personal Reflection

Activity: Spend time writing down two areas of your life that either have been transformed or you wish to be transformed. Then describe how they were transformed or how you think transformation could take place in those areas of life.

Area of Life #1

_____

_____

_____

_____

Area of Life #2

_____

_____

_____

_____

Prayer: Dear Lord, I ask your guidance today as I begin to think more deeply about the areas of my life that need to be transformed, especially areas of my life that may not reflect my Christian heart. I can only hope that through you I may gain the insight and strength to make these changes. I know that living in sync with your expectations will make for a better me. In the name of Jesus Christ, I pray. Amen.

Day 2

Read: Philippians 3

Review: Areas of Life notes from Day 1.

Activity: Take time to expand on the areas in your life you would like to transform. Consider what the barriers might be to those changes. Write down the name of at least one person who could help you overcome those barriers and how he or she could help. Remember that once you have written down one person's name, you immediately have two people, because God is always there. No matter how lonely you may feel, he is there.

Person #1

_____

_____

_____

_____

Person #2

_____

_____

_____

_____

Person #3

_____

_____

_____

_____

Prayer: Dear Lord, please give me the strength to ask others for their assistance in achieving my end result. Allow me to be vulnerable with these people and be protected via our union with you. Let me achieve only that which is good in your presence. Allow my past to be simply that—my past. I welcome a future grounded by your teachings and principles, so that I may be an example of your amazing grace. In the name of Jesus Christ, I pray. Amen.

Day 3

Read: Romans 12

Review: People notes from Day 2.

Activity: We are "living sacrifices" in our walk with God. Each of us is a part of a greater team. Our responsibilities to the communion with God lie in the gifts he has given us. God asks you and me to use our gifts to benefit the whole, not ourselves. With that in mind, answer the following questions:

What gift do you think God has given you? Have you used that gift for yourself or for the benefit of others?

_____

_____

_____

_____

Caring for those that have hurt you is difficult to do. What individuals fall into the "can't deal with" bucket in your life? What will it take to approach them in a Romans 12 way?

_____

_____

_____

_____

Prayer: Dear Lord, be with me as I look into my heart with a new sense of conviction. Allow me to have clarity as to the gifts you have placed with me. Let my needs step aside, as I learn to love purely and help those that might be against me, with reason or not. Show me the greatness that comes from love and not evil. Allow my life to be transformed so that I can accept my enemies through forgiveness and grace. In the name of Jesus Christ, I pray. Amen.

Day 4

Read: 2 Corinthians 3

Review: Gift Answers from Day 3.

Activity: As we grow in our faith with Christ, laws become less of a driving force. Our hearts become filled with the Holy Spirit and this guides our actions. These actions are unveiled and supported by Christ. How different do you feel when your life is directly in line with Christ's wishes or what do you think it would be like?

_____

_____

_____

_____

Prayer: Dear Lord, I ask that my focus will be to gain glory for you and that through this alignment I will bring others around me closer to you. Give me the faith of a servant, knowing that my focus on others ever increases the spirit in my heart. In the name of Jesus Christ, I pray. Amen.

Day 5

Read: Transform

Reflect: Your notes from each of the exercises this week

Activity: Use the space below to summarize the most important transformation that is necessary right now in your life. Create a few action items in order to start focusing on that area. Reach out to the people that can help you. Remember that the effect you have on others will only reach as high as the effect Christ has on you.

_____

_____

_____

_____

Prayer: Dear Lord, please provide me the opportunity for a transformed heart. Allow me to recognize the people in my life that need help. Let me reach out to those that I need help from, so that I don't feel alone. Show me more clearly the gifts you have placed in my heart. I will use them to give glory and honor to your name. In the name of Jesus Christ, I pray. Amen.

Transform—Closing Personal Reflection

A Transformation Story

When you travel only for yourself, the pain will catch up to you at some point in time. Unfortunately, there are many people that are waiting for you to fail. Once the slide begins, your destination is "Rock Bottom." On the way there, you will see one final exit. Will you decide to take it? If so, once on the exit ramp things begin to get even more painful and bleak. You see only one store on that exit. It is an old service station and it is your only chance to refuel for the final leg of your trip.

As you pull up, you realize the pumps are off and the only door is locked. Two empty chairs are out front on the porch with a table between them. You decide to sit, given your exhaustion from the constant running from your pain and suffering. As you sit, you notice a light is shining on a book in the middle of the table between the two chairs. Picking up this curious book, you realize it has your name on the front cover. You begin to rock as you open the cover. Strangely the other chair also begins to rock; yet no one is in the chair.

Startled you gain composure and begin to look at the book's content. Quickly you realize it is a picture book of your life. There are accomplishments, family events, and even a few painful memories. As you get to the most recent pages they are battered and yellow. Then you see the last picture, yet it has not even happened. It is a picture of your car pulling out of the service station. You can hardly tell that it is yours, because it is so broken down and ragged, but it's your license plate for sure. The caption at the bottom of the picture reads: "View from the lens of others."

Blessed are the poor in spirit, for theirs is the kingdom of heaven.

Tears begin to fall from your eyes and hopelessness fills your heart. At that moment the door that was locked slowly swings open and a light comes from within the store. You decide to walk in and the only thing for sale is "Hope" in every imaginable flavor and shape. It's now your choice: Do you ask for that hope or turn and drive into despair? The book in your hand has changed, it is now titled—"Transformation: The greatest gift is hope."

Blessed are those that mourn, for they will be comforted.

The story stops here. God has already given you and me all the tools to write the ending. We all know what we want it to be. Let the transformation necessary in your heart accept the hope it needs. A transformation in any way, shape or form necessary to align more directly with God.

Dreams

Life is a cycle of woulds, coulds, shoulds, ifs, and maybes
Each turn is an opportunity for learning and greatness
We miss some turns in life just because we were not looking
Yet they are always there, around each bend—dreams;

A thought from left field, let go as if no purpose existed
Visions while driving that spark the flame of life, but no action
Tingles of excitement when the future brightens out of darkness
They are happening all around us—see them as they are—dreams;

Life's challenges are like the wind blowing out a candle
The light may be gone briefly; however, all the tools still remain
One small spark is all that is necessary to rekindle the flame
Care for the candle in your life, savor the light cast from your—dreams;

As a small child, life gives you great images of the future
These images are visions of God's plan for each of us
Each view is a fresh opportunity to build upon your purpose
A science project, soccer game, lunch with Dad—samples of dreams;

Morning air provides many opportunities—yet most are missed
Be present to your thoughts and capture the essence of life they bring
Regrets are simply that: moments of time that passed you by
Dreams are moments of time full of color and opportunity—see them.

Living your dreams gives others the hope for their candles.

Dreams—Opening Personal Reflection

Everyone has dreams; some are big and some are very small. Life would seem imperfect without the ability to dream about a new beginning or fresh start. Take hold of these dreams—you never know the impact you may have on others if you live out your dreams. Also remember that some people's dreams may be as simple as a hot meal or a roof over their head. Always dream for those less fortunate than yourself and fulfill smaller dreams for others along the way. Never stop chasing your dreams; God wants us to live a life of passion.

I certainly hope that this week brings you into closer contact with your dreams. Even if significant obstacles stand in the way; keep pushing. Remember what God did in six days. That always puts things into perspective for me.

Associated Scripture Verses

1 Kings 3:5
At Gibeon the Lord appeared to Solomon during the night in a dream, and God said, "Ask for whatever you want me to give you."

Acts 2:17
In the last days, God says, I will pour out my Spirit on all people. Your sons and daughters will prophesy, your young men will see visions, your old men will dream dreams.

Numbers 12:6
...he said, "Listen to my words: "When a prophet of the Lord is among you, I reveal myself to him in visions, I speak to him in dreams.

Day 1

Read: Dreams, Associated Scripture Verses and Opening Personal Reflection

Activity: Spend time reflecting on your current dreams and those you may have left in the past. We seem to quickly let plans and thoughts disappear before we take action. Now you get to be selfish for one day. What have you always wanted? Write down at least two dreams and why they are important to you.

Dream #1

_____

_____

_____

_____

Dream #2

_____

_____

_____

_____

Prayer: Dear Lord, give me the ability to draw closer to you as I explore my dreams. Open my mind to things I never knew were imaginable. The amazing things that you have done give me hope for the thoughts and plans I consider this week. Thank you for life's opportunities. In the name of Jesus Christ, I pray. Amen

Day 2

Read: 1 Kings 3

Review: Dream notes from Day 1

Activity: Yesterday we allowed ourselves to be selfish. Today, we see how God rewards those who act out of compassion for others. Solomon is rewarded with discernment in order to lead others. He thought it was only a dream; yet when he needed that skill the most, it was second nature. Review your dreams from Day 1 and now think about how those dreams can benefit others. See how you can achieve your dreams by making others' dreams come true. Then consider what you would ask for, if God said to you: "Ask for whatever you want me to give you."

Dream #1—Revised

_____

_____

_____

_____

Dream #2—Revised

_____

_____

_____

_____

Response to God and why?

_____

_____

_____

_____

Prayer: Dear Lord, give me the ability to discern right from wrong. Allow my mind to see more of the impact on others, than of the impact on me. Show me ways to satisfy your dreams for me and at the same time fulfill the dreams of those less fortunate than I. In the name of Jesus Christ, I pray. Amen

Day 3

Read: Acts 2

Review: Dream Revision notes from Day 2

Activity: There are times in our lives when we think everyone is speaking a different language, similar to the experience at the Tower of Babel. Then at other points, things become very clear and it feels like we are all together. Acts 2 is a great example of how God can bring us together for the greater good. Describe a time when clarity was obtained regarding a decision as different events started to come together in your life.

Life Situation

_____

_____

_____

_____

Prayer: Dear Lord thank you for the clarity you brought to me through your Son's life. Jesus was given to us in human form to walk with us in our daily lives. Then crucified to save us from sin and offered back to us through the Holy Spirit. Give me the ability to see how things in my life fit together. Thank you for allowing me to dream. In the name of Jesus Christ, I pray. Amen

Day 4

Read: Numbers 12

Review: Life Situation notes from Day 3

Activity: In this chapter of Numbers, God shows us that he can, and does, have direct conversations with people. We sometimes want to make things be about us and think someone else should not be getting everything. Describe a time (be honest) when you were jealous of someone else's status, belongings or achievements. Did that feeling affect anyone else besides you?

Life Experience

_____

_____

_____

_____

Prayer: Dear Lord, please give me a pure heart. Don't let me get caught up in the envy of things occurring in the lives of other people. Remind me that I play a part in your world and clarity will come. Show me in your time and in your way. In the name of Jesus Christ, I pray. Amen

Day 5

Read: Dreams

Reflect: Your notes from each of the exercises this week

Activity: We should never allow life to live us; we should always try to live life. Take one of the dreams you considered this week and write down a few steps you can take to begin making it a reality. Start small, but start. Take into consideration how God has given you this dream.

Dream Plan

_____

_____

_____

_____

Prayer: Dear Lord, open the door for your dreams to come true in my
life. Help me to see the pieces as they fall together. Remove greed
from my mind, so that I can truly experience the dreams that I
never thought were possible. Keep communication lines open
between those in my life that are playing a part in my journey.
Thank you for the ability to look forward regardless of the
situation I am in today. In the name of Jesus Christ, I pray. Amen

Dream—Closing Personal Reflection

We can take a lot from this week, starting with Solomon's desire to help
others, when God had offered to give him "anything." This was followed by the
clarity brought to God's people at Pentecost. Finally, we learn that looking at
ourselves and wondering why we can't be like someone else can cause severe pain.
I have had many dreams in my life. Some were for me, however, more recently
they have been for others.

Once I began writing, clearly my dream was to publish a book. That one has
come true, but it pales in comparison with the dreams that may come true for a
few in an orphanage on another continent. Let me explain: In 2009, I learned,
through my church, of an orphanage in Rwanda, called The Sonrise School.
These children have dreams about things that you and I take for granted every
day. Now by me achieving my goal of publishing this book, I can help make
their dreams come true by donating a portion of the proceeds from each book
sold to this cause.

This is an example of how you can realize your dreams and help
make dreams come true for people you only know through Christ. Good

luck with all your dreams. (To read more about The Sonrise School, go to www.mustardseedproject.org.)

Finally, as I began planning activities around the publishing of this book, I had several dreams. One of them was to speak in Dallas Stadium, as that would show me how successful my book was. Clearly that was my dream; however, as I drew closer to the completion of this book, I realized that the right dream (one from God) would be to fill Dallas Stadium with people that were helped by God through my book. I don't even need to be there, because then it is about me and not about what God wants to do through me. Focus on his dream for you, then and only then will you reach the amazing dreams he has planned for you.

Patience

Did you feel the way you had expected to feel, overwhelmed, scared, excited or surprised?
You waited so long for that time to come—did it meet your expectation—did you have the one?
The person you thought it might be so many times in your head—was she there?
Things just seem to happen some times and you really can't explain it;

So many years have gone by and your hopes and dreams have peaked at every introduction
You wanted to meet that person you thought was coming, but you always second-guessed yourself
Would you be ready? Could you tell if she was the one? Was your past keeping you from her?
One day the right introduction would occur, it would change everything—then it happened;

You knew right away that this was not the normal introduction because the butterflies were there
The way the tea tasted that day was a little better than you remembered from the past
The conversation rolled off your tongue as though you were talking to your best friend
You thought in that small corner of the restaurant something special was happening;

The rest of your day was somewhat normal, except you did not think about this stranger yesterday
Each moment of silence, followed by a mental picture of her and a faint grin—that was new
The days seemed to follow that pattern of thought until you began planning what was next
Yet a continuing question mark of fear and the unforeseen opportunity was in sight;

A few days passed; those butterflies were in full flight and your mind full of questions
Could you have found what you had always thought was there, yet never gave a chance?
Had a few people, all of whom were connected, illuminated a path to your future and happiness?
Could you have just met the woman that would complete every hope and dream?

The next time you met, it was as if you were still in that corner drinking tea and wondering
Kindness was just one of the words that connected you—intrigue was at its full delight
A stranger who had made such an impression, made mere hopes turn to dreams to reality
You only wanted a person, beautiful inside, and for the timing to be right;

There is only one person who knows whether it is right and his Spirit will guide your direction
Your heart is fragile, yet you feel a healing presence through this stranger entering your life
Don't go in without being prepared to feel pain, yet open up and enjoy the new opportunity
Love is a word that is too often used without true understanding of the meaning;

She gives you hope of life to come with happiness, beauty, trust, and companionship
Give all you have when it is time and ensure you love from the inside out—make it unconditional
She makes you smile when alone, dream when driving, plan when flying, and love when right
You met someone that day—was it her?

Be patient and allow God to work in your life.

Associated Scripture Verses

1 Timothy 1:16
But for that very reason I was shown mercy so that in me, the worst of sinners, Christ Jesus might display his unlimited patience as an example for those who would believe on him and receive eternal life.

Isaiah 7:13
Then Isaiah said, "Hear now, you house of David! Is it not enough to try the patience of men? Will you try the patience of my God also?"

Hebrews 6:12
We do not want you to become lazy, but to imitate those who through faith and patience inherit what has been promised.

Patience—Opening Personal Reflection

Relationships are as much a part of life as breathing. They are similar in many ways. When one is not properly functioning, we feel pain and it can truly take over our lives. If you have been in a situation where you were short of breath for whatever reason, I am sure you vowed to never put yourself in that situation again. Having a relationship end with deep pain can have the same effect. We quickly begin to back away from having that pain again. Typically, our loved ones want us to find a new relationship quickly, because they feel that we don't need to be alone and must be happy.

The good thing is we get to still breathe, even though we are not in a relationship. Life without a marriage-type relationship is not the end of life, especially if you are not ready. I simply ask our families and friends to be patient and allow us to heal. God will put the right relationship in your path only when he knows you are ready. When that happens, it will be very clear that you are ready. Your relationship with God is paramount during these times—stay focused.

Day 1

Read: Patience, Associated Scripture Verses and Opening Personal
Reflection

Activity: Spend time thinking about some areas in your life where patience
is very hard to achieve. List at least two areas. Be sure to consider
the "why" you need this "now" as opposed to in God's time.

Area #1

_____

_____

_____

_____

Area #2

_____

_____

_____

_____

Prayer: Dear Lord, protect me as I begin to give up control over some of
my wishes. Show me how patience can make the outcome so much
greater than I ever thought. Watch over those that set expectations
for me, as their frustration may increase as my patience increases.
In the name of Jesus Christ, I pray. Amen

Day 2

Read: 1 Timothy 1

Review: Areas of Patience from Day 1

Activity: Being patient is not very easy. Consider the things we are willing to do in order to get what we want *now*. I think you will clearly see what lack of patience gets you. Take a moment to identify two actions you have taken in your life as shortcuts. Describe the outcome, or the effect on the outcomes, that occurred. (If you are experiencing the joy of a shortcut right now, write that down too, then come back later and note what blew up.) The scary thing is that you might not feel the pain of the shortcut personally. Let me assure you that someone feels it.

Shortcut #1

_____

_____

_____

_____

Shortcut #2

_____

_____

_____

_____

Prayer: Dear Lord, let me learn from my shortcomings and my need-it-now attitudes. Show me the way of Paul as he is rewarded with your grace. Let me have compassion for those that struggle with this way of life. Grant me the skill of patience. In the name of Jesus Christ, I pray. Amen

Day 3

Read: Isaiah 7

Review: Shortcuts from Day 2

Activity: Patience is something we need to have in all aspects of our lives.
Yet, we should never take advantage of someone else's patience. To
do that is as harmful as having no patience for oneself. Outline
two areas or events where you may have used someone else's
patience in a negative, self-fulfilling way.

Patience Area #1

_____

_____

_____

_____

Patience Area #2

_____

_____

_____

_____

Prayer: Dear Lord, ensure that I do not use someone else's patience for
my personal advantage. I know in my heart that patience is a
difficult thing to start with and taking advantage of the innocent
will only challenge my relationship with you. In the name of Jesus
Christ, I pray. Amen

Day 4

Read: Hebrews 6

Review: Patience Area notes from Day 3.

Activity: All around us we see great things happening to people. Yet we
never truly know what they had to go through in order to get
there. As an observer, can you list at least one instance when you
saw patience work in someone else's life? (You may even want to
talk to them about it!)

Instance #1

_____

_____

_____

_____

Instance #2

_____

_____

_____

_____

Prayer: Dear Lord, thank you for the great things that happen on this
earth. Give me perspective, as I look at others who have developed
this great skill. Allow me to gain wisdom from you through
their experiences, as they help me to see firsthand the impact of
discipleship. In the name of Jesus Christ, I pray. Amen

Day 5

Read: Patience

Reflect: Your notes from each of the exercises this week.

Activity: Select one of the areas from Day 1 that you referenced as needing more patience. Use the examples we have read this week to develop a patience game plan for that area and outline that below.

Patience Game Plan

_____

_____

_____

_____

Prayer: Dear Lord, patience is more than a virtue; it is how I honor you with my faith. You have a plan for me and who am I to modify that plan? Create for me the ability to accept patience and prosper through your grace (even though I don't deserve it). In the name of Jesus Christ, I pray. Amen

Patience—Closing Personal Reflection

Patience is one thing we all strive for (and preach), yet is not always displayed or easy to implement. Regardless of what we desire, we always seem to _need it_ right away. Today will not be the same if we don't _get it_ right now. If you can't pay for it, put it on your credit card and pay it off in 3, 6, 12 or 36 months. We have discussed the pain that impatience can cause in our lives. I bet it would not take long to come up with examples from your life.

Only when you realize that great things come in God's time, will patience become easier to accept. After my divorce, I was patient for a while when it came to relationships. At some point, I was not really sure it would ever happen.

I thought at the time I had given up, but what I did was give in to God's will. It was not until I stopped looking for a relationship that God introduced me to my wife on a blind date. Be patient and allow God's will to work in your life.

As a side note, I wrote Patience a couple of days after the blind date with my wife-to-be. I knew it that day. Patience gave me the love of my life. Hang tight and see what it will do for you.

Action

The wind blows and charts an entirely new course for God's creatures
For some the flight path and new landing zone only moved by one branch
Yet others have nothing that was considered theirs a few short hours before
The power of a few moments in time and the forever impacts are amazing;

Never has the middle of any event in life been so important
The ends are squandered away as mere dots in time and unimportant
All that is left is a smash or stroke of sudden realization
This period defines the future and how your actions will mold it forever;

A sprinter prepares for years to take on his challengers in the race of a lifetime
Yet only tenths of a second will determine who crosses the finish line first
The winner could not earn that title without others achieving their purpose
Forever, the two will be joined; the eternal dash starts from there;

The final dot occurs without your involvement or approval of timing
Once you see it coming, only regret may be what is left
Standing on the beach in the eye of a hurricane is how you might feel
The calm is eerie because you have seen the initial fury and know what is next;

God visits your world when you thought it was time to move to his forever
A second chance is what he brings; yet the choice is only yours to decide
The beach is still calm and the eye is your second chance
Trust him blindly, he once parted a sea—the hurricane will be easy.

Take hold of your dash today.

Associated Scripture Verses

2 Corinthians 9:2
For I know your eagerness to help, and I have been boasting about it to the Macedonians, telling them that since last year you in Achaia were ready to give; and your enthusiasm has stirred most of them to action.

James 2:17
In the same way, faith by itself, if it is not accompanied by action, is dead.

Acts 7:22
Moses was educated in all the wisdom of the Egyptians and was powerful in speech and action.

Action—Opening Personal Reflection

The amount of time we have here with our friends and families needs to be used to its fullest. As I mentioned in this writing, there is always a winner, yet without challengers there could not be one. Regardless of which one you are, there is no way anyone could ever say that you did not take action. You always hear that no one remembers who came in second; well, they forgot to ask God.

In today's busy world, we all too often do not reserve time to review the actions we engage in between our birth and death. We especially do not consider thoroughly what our actions may mean to our families in the future. This is probably something many of us do not want to spend time thinking about right now. However, the line between the two dates on our tombstone is all that describes our life, unless we take action now and plan to leave a legacy. I urge you to take time to ponder how you want your great grandchildren to reference you after you have moved to God's heavenly kingdom.

Day 1

Read: Action, Associated Scripture Verses and Opening Personal Reflection section

Activity: Spend time thinking through how you would like to be remembered after your death. Again, not something we consider often. However, if we don't take the time to do this, no course of action can be taken. Make an effort to write down what you want to be remembered by after you mortal life ends.

Your Legacy

_____

_____

_____

_____

Prayer: Dear Lord, give me the strength to take actions that will please you and allow me to leave a legacy my family can be proud of forever. Show me how I can impact those I have never even touched. In the name of Jesus Christ, I pray. Amen

Day 2

Read: 2 Corinthians 9

Review: Legacy notes from Day 1

Activity: Many times in life, we speak of the actions we are going to take, but nothing seems to happen. Talk without action does not glorify God. Think through some of the examples in your life that sound this way. Write down at least two scenarios and how you could get the ball rolling for each.

Scenario #1

_____

_____

_____

_____

Scenario #2

_____

_____

_____

_____

Prayer: Dear Lord, give me the strength to follow through on the actions
            that come from my mouth. Forgive me for the lack of action I
            have displayed in my past. Support me in my desires to move the
            ball forward in each aspect of my life. In the name of Jesus Christ,
            I pray. Amen

Day 3

Read: James 2

Review: Action Scenario notes from Day 1

Activity: Action alone does not make someone a great person. We must
            always consider if the activities we are engaged in are supported
            by the words we say. This is the classic, "Do as I say, not as I do".
            Unfortunately, we all live this way at times. What two actions
            do you need to modify, so they are more in line with your public
            commentary?

Action #1

_____

_____

_____

_____

Action #2

_____

_____

_____

_____

Prayer: Dear Lord, support me as I attempt to treat all of your people in the same manner. Give me the awareness to know when I don't practice what I preach. Show me how to be more true to my values and follow the teachings you provide. In the name of Jesus Christ, I pray. Amen

Day 4

Read: Acts 7

Review: Action notes from Day 3

Activity: As you read in Acts 7, many actions were taken by several different people, all for God. If God were to ask you to do something that did not seem logical based on your thoughts, would you do it? Describe either a scenario you have experienced or someone you know who had a similar situation occur. Was the outcome what was expected?

Experience

_____

_____

_____

_____

Prayer: Dear Lord, allow me to learn from the actions your disciples have taken on your behalf. Prepare my heart for unquestioned action to fulfill the needs of your people. Give me the strength to trust all that you put in my path. In the name of Jesus Christ, I pray. Amen

Day 5

Read: Action

Reflect: Your notes from each of the exercises this week.

Activity: This week we began discussing how we want to be remembered by our families. At a minimum, we now understand that this can't happen without taking certain actions. Create an action plan for yourself to solidify your legacy. List as many actions as you wish, but do start. Begin that journey. Be true to yourself.

Action Planning

_____

_____

_____

_____

Prayer: Dear Lord, allow me to implement the thoughts you place on my heart. Show me how I can leave a legacy for my family, friends and community. Thank you for assisting me with the imprint I will leave on your people. In the name of Jesus Christ, I pray. Amen

Action—Closing Personal Reflection

Taking action is one of the simplest things to do in our lives. The problem is that we can do a lot of things, but do they really mean anything? I saw a YouTube video recently of Derek Redmond that proves how much a single action can impact everyone. If you have not seen it, do a search on YouTube to find and view it. Derek was expected to win the 400m in the 1992 Olympics, but pulled up during the race due to a hamstring injury.

The injury should have been the end of the story; however, that is just the beginning. After being down on the track for a brief period, he gets up and tries to hobble to the finish line. As he makes his way there, clearly in severe pain, his father comes from the stands to help him get to the end. Just before the finish line, his father lets go so that his son can finish what he started. As he crosses the line, he receives a standing ovation from over 65,000 people.

The point here is to finish strong and never give up. I don't even know who won that race, but I know all I need to know as it pertains to life. What a legacy!! Take action to make it clear what your life was all about!

Fearful

Your pain makes it feel so insincere and unbelievable
Previous hurt and actions will not let you think or feel it is true
It might be, yet how could it be; no one ever let it be real for me
How could it happen and why is now the right time?

Life has thrown so many curve balls that the process is just a game
However, his sincerity rolls like water off a leaf on a rainy day
I think for a minute I can catch that drop and it still be moist
Am I dreaming, or is it reality? And this person, is he real?

He seems so open and ready to provide what I thought was fake
My heart says yes, but my intuition says I have been here before
My steps are forward, but my mind is backwards—not ready for yet another detour
Could I be turning down the feelings I always thought I wanted;

I have so much to give and provide to the right person
Been there before, and it was a dream that was woken by a nightmare
Someone said it would change, yet the nightmare started all over again
Will I let this new person into my heart and open up for another hurt?

Sometimes you have to let a larger force control your reactions
If I am scared, let it go—why should more pain be cast?
Be prepared if you go forward because he may change your life
His heart is in the right place, but the timing could be all wrong;

At some point you will love again, it might not be now
Enjoy the companionship, but be sure not to pass along your confusion and pain
Could you be ready and not know it? Yes, but your actions speak louder than words
He is ready for you, are you ready for him?

A cycle was created and you happen to be in it, the pain deafening
He was not a part of it, so be careful not to make him pay the price
His heart is full of love and compassion, ready to be spread like nectar on a spring day
Be honest with yourself and let him know.

Associated Scripture Verses

Leviticus 26:36
As for those of you who are left, I will make their hearts so fearful in the lands of their enemies that the sound of a windblown leaf will put them to flight. They will run as though fleeing from the sword, and they will fall, even though no one is pursuing them.

Deuteronomy 28:59
. . . the Lord will send fearful plagues on you and your descendants, harsh and prolonged disasters, and severe and lingering illnesses.

Isaiah 35:4
. . . say to those with fearful hearts, "Be strong, do not fear; your God will come, he will come with vengeance; with divine retribution he will come to save you."

Fearful—Opening Personal Reflection

Our experiences can change how we perceive the world and trust those around us. Fear is one of the feelings that can take the breath right out of us. When these events are very personal in nature, the pain and fear is taken to another level. As life changes for each of us, we need to ensure that we focus on the impact each experience has on our lives. We need to take the good and leave the bad behind. Learn from the experience, yet not carry it with us. Fear keeps us from moving on and can sometimes be the stumbling block we never see. If we fear anything, we should fear letting God down by our actions. This fear is one of "not living" like we know we should.

The fear is real in many scenarios, yet we must control how we respond, because either we hurt others in the process or we miss out on great opportunities. We must learn to take lessons from our past, but certainly keep living.

Day 1

Read: Fearful, Associated Scripture Verses and Opening Personal Reflection

Activity: Think back on a situation in your life when you were timid regarding a decision due to past failures or pains. Did that timidity keep you from taking action? How have you handled fear in your life? Describe two times in your life where fear changed, stalled or impacted a decision.

Decision #1

_____

_____

_____

_____

Decision #2

_____

_____

_____

_____

Prayer: Dear Lord, allow me to learn from the places of fear in my life. Remind me that you are always there for me and that I am never alone. Ensure that I don't let my fear hurt other people indirectly. In the name of Jesus Christ, I pray. Amen

Day 2

Read: Leviticus 26

Review: Decision notes from Day 1

Activity: This chapter of Leviticus is difficult to read given the anger represented through what we typically characterize as a loving

God. We must remember that the Old Testament fear came from not following God's ways and commandments. None of us are perfect and we make mistakes. Describe why you think God used fear to teach his people in this situation and how it might apply to your life today?

Fear of God

_____

_____

_____

_____

Prayer: Dear Lord, give me a better understanding of fear and how that fear closes so many doors in my life. Show me how fear can be taken away by your forgiveness of past sins. We are all so broken and sin is always among us. Thank you for your unending forgiveness. In the name of Jesus Christ, I pray. Amen

Day 3

Read: Deuteronomy 28

Review: Fear of God notes from Day 2

Activity: At this point, you are probably saying: Why so much fear from a loving God? One of the great outcomes of this discussion is that living in line with God's teaching helps us understand the fear of him more clearly. Sometimes it takes this realization to change someone's perspective and behavior. Describe below how a time of fear has changed your life in a positive way.

Changed by Fear

_____

_____

_____

_____

Prayer: Dear Lord, some of the experiences we have in life teach us the impacts of living for ourselves. And the outcomes help us get more centered on you. These changes are an outward sign that the love you offer is so much greater than any fear we have. In the name of Jesus Christ, I pray. Amen

Day 4

Read: Isaiah 35

Review: Changed by Fear notes from Day 3

Activity: Hopefully this chapter gives you a sense of how great God is for those that believe in him. We see that the difficult or unpleasant things that God may allow in our lives are in order to protect his believing community. Describe how this chapter changed your understanding of fear related to God.

Fear and God

_____

_____

_____

_____

Prayer: Dear Lord, you bring clarity at all the right times. We realize fear
            of you is what gives us protection in your kingdom. You truly
            are the great God and we stand strong against any fear that does
            not come from you. You are our protector. In the name of Jesus
            Christ, I pray. Amen

Day 5

Read: Fearful

Reflect: Your notes from each of the exercises this week

Activity: We have read how scary God can be and seen how great he can be.
            If we only had the Old Testament as God's word, things would
            be a lot different in the way we approach God. However, the New
            Testament offers a loving God, who no longer rules by fear, but
            love and forgiveness. Understanding this shift is paramount. How
            would you respond if a non-believer asks you. "How can you love
            a God that asks you to fear him?"

Love, Fear and God

_____

_____

_____

_____

Prayer: Dear Lord, give me the words to help others understand how fear
            can be turned into opportunity. Show me the way to a productive
            life. Let me learn from my moments of fear and allow me to
            overcome those challenges with your help. In the name of Jesus
            Christ, I pray. Amen

Fearful—Closing Personal Reflection

My being fearful almost prevented this book from ever being written. My gift from God was writing and I guess it had to be poetry. Poetry is really not the standard topic of conversation on the first tee of a Saturday morning golf outing, but it is my gift. At one point, I was very concerned about how people would respond to me writing poetry. I was a high school football player, college fraternity guy and, yes, I have had my share of poker nights. His gift does not fit into any of these activities very well at all. Plain and simple, I was fearful of what people would say about me.

I had it all wrong. Once *I* figured that out, or maybe it was the third two-by-four that God popped me with—ok—fine God allowed me to figure it out. This book is about what people are gaining from God through my writings. It's about the impacts I see happen in many people and scenarios. Remember God changed my life at a golf tournament, so why can't we talk about God on the first tee or at a football game? What happens when someone gets hurt at a football game? We pray. It's not about my poetry—it's about God's word.

My fear has lead to amazing opportunities. Understanding God's word helps me to embrace those opportunities that he provides.

Gift

You have waited to receive it for many years
The work you put forth ensured that you were deserving
Yet it slipped away several times, because it was not time
Emotions sit strong and quickly when the outcome is not your expected gift;

Our expectations are formed through thoughts of our plans
Letting go of your plan and accepting blind travel is difficult
A piano player without sight never sees the path of his hands across the keys
The resulting music is amazing as it flows from his gift;

A new path in life comes out of your assumed missed opportunity
One that led to an intersection with God, our Creator
This encounter is where I and he merge together forever
His timing and plan will still feel foreign, which is a gift;

Life provides direction for us to take. God is there
We can accept them or travel down the path of "why"
That trip will have pain and suffering, given we choose the path
Accepting his will and way creates happy trails to his gift;

The gift of life is essential to ensure God's plan for us all
Two of his creations meet at the intersection of life
Once together, they emerge as a new beginning with purpose
A child is born by God's will, and we receive our gift.

Associated Scripture Verses

Romans 6:23
For the wages of sin is death, but the gift of God is eternal life in Christ Jesus our Lord.

James 1:17
Every good and perfect gift is from above, coming down from the Father of the heavenly lights, who does not change like shifting shadows.

Revelation 22:17
The Spirit and the bride say, "Come!" And let him who hears say, "Come!" Whoever is thirsty, let him come; and whoever wishes, let him take the free gift of the water of life.

Gift—Opening Personal Reflection

Many couples struggle with having children. It seems so easy and "natural," but fertilization does not happen as simply as expected. There are many medical reasons why this may be the case, yet at other times, "It just did not work," is all that remains. Thousands of dollars are spent to try multiple procedures, and the outcome is still empty. In God's time and way, our gift will come to us, and it might not be what we expected. Be careful with expectations, as they can let you down.

God's gifts come in many forms and children are only one of his great gifts. It is important that we embrace these gifts as they are truly through the Holy Spirit. Don't be surprised by what God puts in our lives.

Day 1

Read: Gifts, Associated Scripture Verses and Opening Personal Reflection

Activity: Gifts from God come in so many different ways. We must keep our awareness level on high when we walk with God. He sometimes whispers to you only so that you can grasp your gift more clearly over time. What gift has God placed in your life and what might he want you to do with this gift?

Gift from God

_____

_____

_____

_____

Prayer: Dear Lord, please give me the insight to understand the ways you are gifting me. Ensure that I know the gift or gifts are for your benefit, not mine. Clear my mind of the daily clutter, so your thoughts may guide my action. Thank you for the impact you have on my life and the calmness you bring to others. In the name of Jesus Christ, I pray. Amen

Day 2

Read: Romans 6

Review: Gift from God notes from Day 1

Activity: We are taught that in order to receive, we must first give. We have given our lives to Christ in order to receive the gift of eternal life. How do you live out this principle in your life?

Life given to Christ

_____

_____

_____

_____

Prayer: Dear Lord, show me that giving of myself is the most important thing I can do for you and your kingdom. Allow me to realize just how much the gift of my time means to my family. Fill my heart with the spirit, so that I may understand my path more clearly. In the name of Jesus Christ, I pray. Amen

Day 3

Read: James 1

Review: Life Given to Christ notes from Day 2

Activity: There are plenty of definitions for the word "gift." We can have monetary, physical, or spiritual gifts, among many more. Typically when we think of gifts, the primary focus is what to buy or what we want. What does James say about the origins of the perfect and right gifts?

Origin of Gifts

_____

_____

_____

_____

Prayer: Dear Lord, give me the strength to take direction and not create my own ideas for guidance, unless they are from you. Allow me a peek into the life that comes through you. Bless those who follow your teachings. Your gifts for me are plentiful. Show me how to protect and share them. In the name of Jesus Christ, I pray. Amen

Day 4

Read: Revelation 22

Review: Origin of Gifts notes from Day 3

Activity: Christ died. Christ has risen. Christ will come again. As we continue to see that our real gifts are from God, we will want to do so much with those gifts. Describe what the day Christ returns would look like for you if it were to happen in your lifetime. Take into consideration the feeling you would have immediately after hearing "Well done, my Faithful Servant."

The Meeting

_____

_____

_____

_____

Prayer: Dear Lord, give me the strength to face my fears of acceptance and the humility to accept your gift of living water. I am nothing without what you have predestined for me. May my gifts encourage others and strengthen my relationship with you. In the name of Jesus Christ, I pray. Amen

Day 5

Read: Gift

Reflect: Your notes from each of the exercises this week.

Activity: Regardless of where you are in your life right now, God has a gift growing inside you. It is not imperative that you know what your gift is; only that you know there is one. Keep the faith and always know that it is God who gives the gift, in his time and in his way. How has this week changed your thoughts about gifts?

Gift Changes

_____

_____

_____

_____

Prayer: Dear Lord, offer me the opportunity to see your gifts in your
time. Prepare my heart for the acceptance of your gifts and the
determination to implement them as you see fit. I thank you so
much for the opportunity to experience this through you. In the
name of Jesus Christ, I pray. Amen

Gift—Closing Personal Reflection

The simple fact that we are here, walking with God each day is a gift.
Receiving a material present from someone is really a very small piece of the
"gift equation" in our spiritual life. We are all born with special gifts placed by
God. Now, I am sure some of you are saying, "I don't have one." Well, it may
just be that the time to reveal your gift has not come. God has a very specific
timetable for gifting and we don't get a say on when, only the opportunity to
accept His gracious gift.

I realize we have already spent a week on patience, but that is a constant
theme in God's world. Many people are aware they have something special and
expect immediate returns. Sorry, but it typically does not work that way. Be
patient and allow God to fully develop your gift over time. Once he has done
that and you have shown great patience, the result can be simply amazing. Also
know that it may be hard for others to see it or understand it. However, that is
exactly the point; we are all different and gifted in our own unique ways.

The ability to write only came to me in 2003, as time progressed and my
faith became much stronger. God began to show me different aspects of writing.
It was not until 2010 when it all came together. Have patience for your gift to be
realized. When God does show you the full picture, don't ask questions … Go!

Determination

The sun rises and sets each day as the case has been for all my years
Dreams and plans coat the rays of light with glistening flare
Clarity of the soul only exceeded by the visibility of the day
Your life has come together so well and your heart is full of determination;

A glimmer of pain starts a confusing chain reaction of fear and concern
Every step so well planned out, seems to quickly collapse
Those around you are at full attention, even the youngest is aware
The setback is medically real; yet, my plans are still there to complete—determined;

New flesh is given to bring new life and rescue your hopes for the future
Disregard for one's own life gave years to your friends and family
Life, now different, is moving from this experience with a new sense of grace
Your reason for being has changed like the leaves of the fall—much more determined;

The energy spent to care for those around you is clear to the eye
One that was simply taking from that care, feels a brush from the Holy Spirit
As the night was quickly moving to dawn, the end was much closer than known
Yet God's hand walked the young one to your side with amazed determination;

Many days, months and years flowed by, as more time was granted by our Creator
The impacts from your life on others pop up like flowers at a new home
You have now moved to be with all those who watched over you all those years.
Amazing is what you are and the gifts you left behind is all that I can determine.

Be determined to carry on the legacy that was given to you by loved ones.

Associated Scripture Verses

Psalm 147:4
He determines the number of the stars and calls them each by name.

1 Corinthians 12:11
All these are the work of one and the same Spirit, and he gives them to each one, just as he determines.

Acts 17:26
From one man he made every nation of men, that they should inhabit the whole earth; and he determined the times set for them and the exact places where they should live.

Determination—Opening Personal Reflection

If you have ever been around a person who seems to walk through every bad situation with grace and determination, then you clearly understand God's disciples. When my father was still young, his life changed due to kidney disease and he ultimately required a kidney transplant. We are talking about the mid 1970s, so it was not the most common procedure. However, God had already determined the donor; it was his sister Katherine who gave him a kidney. That gift gave me a father, and for that I can truly never be thankful enough.

The remaining thirty-plus years of his life were sometimes a daily challenge, but most would never have known it. He was determined to live fully, take care of his family at any cost, serve his community and customers and be the best husband, father, brother, and friend possible. Finally, he was a great servant leader. His actions were always for someone else and never selfish. I miss him every day, but I am determined to carry on his legacy. To Katherine: I thank you with all my heart!! You showed me that our lives are not important unless we are changing the lives of others. Wow, did you do that or what!

Day 1

Read: Determination, Associated Scripture Verses and Opening Personal Reflection

Activity: There are two definitions for determination that I want us to explore. The first definition is "something that is already decided" and the other is "your mindset when tackling a job." How do you think God uses both those in your relationship with him?

Determination—Already Decided

_____

_____

_____

_____

Determination—Mindset

_____

_____

_____

_____

Prayer: Dear Lord, offer me a heart of determination. Don't let me ever give up, regardless of the valleys I must cross. My challenges are only opportunities to further my relationship with you. Thank you for the wisdom to guide my life. In the name of Jesus Christ, I pray. Amen

Day 2

Read: Psalm 147

Review: Determination—Already Decided/ Mindset notes from Day 1

Activity: This Psalm uses "determine" in the sense that God is in control of things. This effectively means that we are not. (Yes, I said that!) Yet we live every day trying to control nearly everything in our lives. Describe how you could live a more "God determined" life and what sacrifices you may have to make.

God Determined

_____

_____

_____

_____

Prayer: Dear Lord, take my desires and my outcomes away from the plan I think I have. Show me the way you have already determined for me. Allow me to see how much easier it is without the every day fight. Protect me as I give up control. In the name of Jesus Christ, I pray. Amen

Day 3

Read: Acts 17

Review: God Determined notes from Day 2

Activity: Again, we see the definition of determine as something that God does for us. However, consider for a minute the determination (definition #2) his disciples must have had. They never gave up, even when they were run out of Thessalonica. Do you have that kind of determination in your life? If so, describe the situation. If not, is there an area of your life where you should have that type of determination, but for whatever reasons you have actively chosen not to give the effort? What is that like?

Life Determination

_____

_____

_____

_____

Prayer: Dear Lord, Thank you for the challenges given to me, so that I might look deeper into what is important in my life. Give me the strength to mold into your way as I see my path through your eyes. In the name of Jesus Christ, I pray. Amen

Day 4

Read: 1 Corinthians 12

Review: Life Determination notes from Day 3

Activity: The body is the core theme of this chapter. Here, we read about two different types of bodies, our earthly body and the body of believers (as we are referred to as a collective group following Christ). How do these two definitions work together in your life? Are they both healthy?

Contrasting Bodies

_____

_____

_____

_____

Prayer: Dear Lord, I pray for the health of both bodies. I ask for clarity, since I realize that when my earthly body is unhealthy, I turn to you, just as your greater body turns to you when in despair. Heal us with forgiveness and compassion for we have given our lives to you. In the name of Jesus Christ, I pray. Amen

Day 5

Read: Determination

Reflect: Your notes from each of the exercises this week.

Activity: Describe how your determination to live a God-focused life has changed this week. Consider the understanding that God determines the outcome; not you, and how that might impact the discussion.

Determination Changes

_____

_____

_____

_____

Prayer: Dear Lord, I pray for a life guided by your principles and focused on your choices for me. Don't allow changes in my life's path to scare me; only make me more determined to make adjustments, given I know those changes are from you. In the name of Jesus Christ, I pray. Amen

Determination—Closing Personal Reflection.

This book is truly a reflection of both definitions of determination. I fully believe that God set out for me to write this book. If I did not think that, the effort spent to get to this point would have been a waste of time. That is impossible because of what I have learned about myself, and many others, throughout this journey. I will not find out for sure if God determined this book for me till later in life. However, given you are reading this, I believe I am beginning to see the answer.

Earlier in my life, I clearly never thought anything like this was possible. I would ask you to embrace new things in your life that occur without much explanation. That could in fact be a clear sign of its origin. I would also suggest that you not go looking for your gift, it will find you. The more closely you align yourself with God, the more clear it may become.

Finally, the second definition of determination is on nearly every page of this book. There have been many instances and life situations that could have easily derailed this effort. A few of them slowed the process, yet I was unwilling to let them affect the outcome. I am absolutely determined to impact other people's lives in a positive way through the gifts God has provided me. Don't let yourself get in the way, instead accept what has been determined, and apply every ounce of determination you have to follow your gift.

Comfort

Things occur in life that provide no explanation or reason
Thoughts and happenings are so far from reality, yet are there
He was my rock and future that I built emotions upon
God had a plan that I was completely unaware of and still not understanding;

I reflect this day on a life that was taken too early
Dreams shattered in the midst of what was a normal day
Plans that were changed at the spur of a moment
Hope for a life full of memories that are now pictures and stories that fill the time;

My faith has led me to accept the harsh actions of life
Realizing that there are not answers to all of life's events
Even the pleasures that lie ahead are completely foreign at the moment
God's way provides hope and realization of the peace to come;

I reflect on the horses, so much a part of his life
The saddle of life that I am left to ride upon
Yet the tears flow like rain on the trail we used to ride together
Now he is there watching and guiding you on a daily basis;

Our thoughts distracted today by the pain that dwells within us
Look deep for the meaning that his life provided you and others
The years to come will provide growth opportunities now so distant from thought
His departure, so terrible, will shed the grace of angels and brightness of stars to your life;

How can I feel solace in such a time of pain and misunderstanding?
Am I to move on, acting as if it did not happen?
Sit in my pain and let it rule my life and ruin what he wanted for me?
He sits at the foot of our Lord now, making decisions and helping your every feeling;

As hard as it might be to lift my head and face the future
His life was not given in vain, and peace will cover my heart in time
Allow me to understand and build a house for him within
A place for his memories to grow and desires to be fulfilled through my actions;

My life is not forever on earth, but will grow with love that never leaves the heart
He will be with you every moment both night and day supporting you
You provided all you had for him as he grew and now that growth is with God
How could anyone provide a life full of more peace, happiness and commitment.

Comfort now lives in God's hands.

Associated Scripture Verses

Psalm 23:4
Even though I walk through the valley of the shadow of death, I will fear no evil, for you are with me; your rod and your staff, they comfort me.

Isaiah 61:2
... to proclaim the year of the Lord's favor and the day of vengeance of our God, to comfort all who mourn ...

Matthew 5:4
Blessed are those who mourn, for they will be comforted.

Comfort—Opening Personal Reflection

Many years ago, I was part of a small group discussing losses we had experienced and accepting the healing God was providing to our hearts. One of the group members tragically lost her son. He was murdered. I can't tell you the pain that she was experiencing. This poem is a reflection of that time and the hopelessness that not only she felt, but that you could clearly see and feel. Even in those deepest of sorrows, always remember that God is with you. Have comfort knowing that God will stand firm for you through the hardest of times. He just asks that we stand firm for him in our greatest of times. We all will go through painful periods in our lives and a complete understanding of "why" will not be there. Reach out to God and lift up your pain. Do not ever feel like you have to do it alone or that hope for the future is gone.

Day 1

Read: Comfort, Associated Scripture Verses and Opening Personal Reflection

Activity: Death is very real and so are all the emotions that surround it, especially when that death is sudden, unexplainable or intentional. We really have no one to turn to but God. Describe how God helps to comfort us in our times of need, even though he does not, in these kinds of situations, reveal all the details of 'why'?

Comforting God

_____

_____

_____

_____

Prayer: Dear Lord, help us to understand why not immediately getting all the answers to a painful event is good. Show us the value of comfort in our times of need and allow us to comfort others. We offer patience to you, knowing that one day we will understand the "whys" of life. In the name of Jesus Christ, I pray. Amen

Day 2

Read: Psalm 23

Review: Comforting God notes from Day 1

Activity: Clearly we hear this passage read at nearly all the funerals we attend. God will comfort us through the valley of the shadow of death. Knowing that God's kingdom is eternal and this world is temporary, do you fear death? Describe that fear. What does it mean to you?

Fear of Death

_____

_____

_____

_____

Prayer: Dear Lord, prepare us with a heart of understanding, in order for us to grasp death more firmly. Show us that the movements you make are for a greater purpose. Console us through a painful time, when many of us question things that happen and anger sometimes fills our hearts. Confirm this emotion as only a part of the mourning process and give us strength to rebound. In the name of Jesus Christ, I pray. Amen

Day 3

Read: Isaiah 61

Review: Fear of Death notes from Day 2

Activity: God can truly allow great things to come out of very bad situations. We sometimes hear that an event in our lives is a learning experience. It never makes sense when we are living with the pain, but we always seem to grow. Why do you think God uses times of suffering to teach us so many lessons and show such amazing grace?

Learning Moments

_____

_____

_____

_____

Prayer: Dear Lord, the pain is so great sometimes, yet your comfort helps to ease the emotions. Help me understand the lessons from each of life's experiences, in your time. Remind me it is a necessary part of life and growth. In the name of Jesus Christ, I pray. Amen

Day 4

Read: Matthew 5

Review: Learning Moments notes from Day 3

Activity: In this chapter, we see the Beatitudes and also a discussion of divorce, adultery, and murder, among other things. Death is defined as the end of something; not necessarily life, but perhaps an emotional death. Describe an experience in your life that was an emotional death to you, something that caused significant loss and how Matthew 5 helped you better understand.

Significant Loss

_____

_____

_____

_____

Prayer: Dear Lord, give us the strength to understand the need for painful situations during our lifetime. Reinforce in our hearts the feeling of reconciliation and forgiveness. Allow us to show appreciation even for the bad times, as we learn so much during those periods. In the name of Jesus Christ, I pray. Amen

Day 5

Read: Comfort

Reflect: Your notes from each of the exercises this week.

Activity: Explain how this week has prepared you for times of hardship. How differently will you approach death and the comfort necessary to heal and forgive in the future? Base that not only on your thoughts this week, but also on real deaths that have occurred in your life..

_____

_____

_____

_____

Prayer: Dear Lord, you give and you take away from us. Allow us to see the growth that is left behind. This view will certainly give us a greater appreciation and also offer a better understanding for the days to come. We know that great things are coming. Please do not let us give up. In the name of Jesus Christ, I pray. Amen.

Comfort—Closing Personal Reflection

Watching someone grieve for a loved one is probably the hardest thing I have ever done. Words do not seem to make the emotions disappear, only subside for a few moments. I have never met the person on whom this writing was based. His mother is truly a great person. Even though we have not spoken in some time, I think of her often. Losing a child is something I have never experienced and hope I never do. Losing someone at such a young age via an act of violence is heart wrenching. Just know that regardless of the situation, God is there to comfort you.

I encourage you, and anyone you know, to take the time to process death with God and others around you. Don't let the feelings and thoughts you have stay inside; get them out. This process is not always easy, but don't allow one death to create an emotional death within you.

Remember, you have purpose and the person you mourn for had one too. Live with passion for the new purposes that might come from your pain. Allow God to provide the comfort. You provide the determination to live according to his will.

Vision

Our meals happen each day, because that is what is expected or normal
Those that cherish a single meal don't see from the same lens
Amazement is what we may think; humble is how they feel
Strength gives opportunity to the garden of life; sow the seeds of God;

A home provides shelter from the ills of nature allowing comfort inside
The draping of palm leaves is all that separates some from those same ills
Safety is a feeling behind our walls; fear of what tomorrow brings is their thought
Comfort is the place where shelters are built for those in need;

The completion of a book brings new guidance to our lives
Clarity of what this paper does or what the markings mean is so foreign
The separate meanings are a sign of how far we still have to go
Achievement is only the opportunity to pass along learning to a wanting soul;

A gift received brings complete joy and excitement to a child's face
A stream of clean water, only out-sparkled by the eye of a thirsty child
Both draw similar emotions, yet no comparison is even fair
A month to view your needs in a mirror may be the reflection of a lifetime;

Challenges are only as big as we allow them to be in our lives
Keep grounded—our expectations might be another's lifelong dream
Living for a greater purpose gives insight to the realities of one's impact
Our paths are full of visions; be sure to keep your perspective.

Associated Scripture Verses

Daniel 4:13
In the visions I saw while lying in my bed, I looked, and there before me was a messenger, a holy one, coming down from heaven.

Ezekiel 13:23
... therefore you will no longer see false visions or practice divination. I will save my people from your hands. And then you will know that I am the Lord.

Hosea 12:10
I spoke to the prophets, gave them many visions and told parables through them.

Vision—Opening Personal Reflection

How we view the world is very different from person to person. A necessity for one person could very easily be something never used, or even thrown away, by another person. We are extremely diverse as a country and world; yet collectively we can do great things. We need to ensure that we take time to understand each other and what drives our uniqueness. I assure you that without everyone doing his or her part, from God's perspective, we will never truly achieve our purpose as a country or a world. Always listen to the opinions of others and try to understand their point of view. It could possibly change yours forever. "Just because" is not an acceptable vision from anyone.

Day 1

Read: Vision, Associated Scripture Verses and Opening Personal Reflection.

Activity: We are all unique and many of us see the same thing in different ways. As you explore how blessed you are, think about how you view your life. Do you take things for granted? For example: When you throw away something that has yet to be worn out, do you think of those that only wish they had that choice?

Taken for Granted

_____

_____

_____

_____

Prayer: Dear Lord, thank you for the opportunities you have placed in my life. Show me how to help those less fortunate in your way. Help me to think through the needs of others and provide all that I can—not just to my neighbors, but also those that might not eat today. In the name of Jesus Christ, I pray. Amen

Day 2

Read: Daniel 4

Review: Taken for Granted notes from Day 1

Activity: In this chapter we see how selfishly building yourself up can lead to a tough ending. God wants us to prosper, yet we always must understand it in terms of his kingdom, not ours. We have an obligation to take care of his people. Do you care for God's children or are you building your own kingdom?

Care or Build

_____

_____

_____

_____

Prayer: Dear Lord, show me how to help others with more of an impact. Keep me from focusing on me too much. Use your light to guide me in the right direction. Speak to me so that I may understand more clearly. Focus me, so that I may live a life of servanthood. In the name of Jesus Christ, I pray. Amen

Day 3

Read: Ezekiel 13

Review: Care or Build notes from Day 2

Activity: Interpretation can be a dangerous thing in life, especially when we take that information and attempt to predict the future. In our jobs, we sometimes attempt to forecast future events; however, in our work with the Lord, only he can truly see the future. When you spend time looking forward in your life, how many times are others involved? Don't we typically say: "in 5 years, I want to be …?" Describe how following God's vision, not ours, would play out in your life.

Following God's Plan

_____

_____

_____

_____

Prayer: Dear Lord, protect me from predicting the future and allow me to live more by your calling. Don't let me provide false plans for others to gain more for me. Remind me to direct others to you for the outcomes. In the name of Jesus Christ, I pray. Amen

Day 4

Read: Hosea 12

Review: Following God's Plan notes from Day 3

Activity: In this passage from Hosea, we are reminded that God has visions for us and he controls our lives. In the story of Jacob and Esau, what we see are Jacob's less than aboveboard actions: his trickery, lies, and deceit. Yet we also see God's vision for him played out through his covenant with Abraham. Describe a time when the things you saw people do did not line up with the great outcome they received. How can good things happen to people that seemingly do bad things?

Good from Bad

_____

_____

_____

_____

Prayer: Dear Lord, prepare my heart to not be judgmental of others. I only see what is outward; never do I understand the vision you have for another person or what is growing in his or her heart through you. Give me understanding, so that I may see more clearly the outcome and not just the actions. In the name of Jesus Christ, I pray. Amen

Day 5

Read: Vision

Reflect: Your notes from each of the exercises this week.

Activity: We have talked a lot this week about God's vision for us. I would like for you to consider how other people view you. Typically, what others think is not important, yet when you live one way and talk another way, you can send the wrong message to new followers of Jesus Christ. How do you think others view your life?

View from Others

_____

_____

_____

_____

Prayer: Dear Lord, guide my actions by your dreams, not mine. Ensure that I live a life that is in line with what I say. Don't let mixed signals come from my actions. Be with me always and protect me through the challenges of life. In the name of Jesus Christ, I pray. Amen.

Vision – Closing Personal Perspective

This writing is very important for me because of what the underlying theme represents. Many people in this world at this exact moment don't know where their next meal will come from. Yet my pantry has food in it that sits waiting. Others will not have a cover over their homes for years to come. I live in a home that keeps danger at arms length. I am simply grateful for what I have and saddened by what others have to go through daily.

Just as we can't understand why no food exists for them, they may also wonder why we take so much for ourselves and don't share. I implore you to help those in need, regardless of what they need. Find a way. It's God's vision for each of us to help. There are many ways to help; money is not the only way. Give of your time, for this changes hearts. Money only changes hands, it's completely unemotional. I have dedicated a portion of the proceeds from this book to help those in need. As encouraging as the writing process has been, I think the most rewarding part is yet to come, when I can help implement the actions, which will help those less fortunate. For you, it may be something totally different. The important thing is that you help others in any way you can.

Desire

The powerful emotion of life that drives the heart to respond
It makes little reactions seem like a volcano that is ready to explode
Complete willingness to let past hurt see the darkness of a locked room
Ready to share and open up for what God has prepared for you;

A single reflection becomes the target of heartfelt verbiage
Nothing you do is complete without the acceptance of her voice
She makes you create warmth that a winter snow can't touch
A new budding flower is growing within you and spring is in sight;

Let it go and don't hold it within, because the feeling is so true
You may want to temper the fear, yet driving emotion lets it out
Why not explore what your heart is pouring out, but your conscience holds in?
She is what you have always wanted, yet drives complete confusion;

A place that allows confusion and satisfaction to coexist and create the next move
A move that is somewhat different, yet seems like an old habit, ready to react
This feeling that provides decisions without thinking of the impact
Your heart pounds like the winds of a hurricane, but offer the calm of the eye;

Make progress and don't let your fear keep you from happiness
If it is wrong, then the outcome will take care of itself
If it is right, things will surpass even your greatest of dreams
She is the complete package of beauty and inner peace that supports your every move;

Why have you been so fearful of your emotions that seem so right?
Allow the movement of your heart to connect with hers, exceeded only by God's patience
Plow through the fear and plant the seeds of growth, where all happiness will blossom
Let it go—opportunity sits beside you and is knocking on your door.

Can you answer desire?

Associated Scripture Verses

1 Chronicles 29:18
O Lord, God of our fathers Abraham, Isaac and Israel, keep this desire in the hearts of your people forever, and keep their hearts loyal to you.

Ecclesiastes 12:5
... when men are afraid of heights and of dangers in the streets; when the almond tree blossoms and the grasshopper drags himself along and desire no longer is stirred. Then man goes to his eternal home and mourners go about the streets.

Isaiah 55:11
... so is my word that goes out from my mouth: It will not return to me empty, but will accomplish what I desire and achieve the purpose for which I sent it.

Desire—Opening Personal Reflection

Desire creates excitement in the minds and hearts of thousands each day. Without this emotion, I am pretty sure much that started as a great idea, would still be just a great idea. This emotion starts deep inside and motivates us to do things, ask for things, and say things that we have never said before. Now, stop for a second. Does what you are doing benefit not only yourself, but others as well? Both are fine—just don't confuse them. What is good for you is not always good for the collective whole. Always consider others and have the grand desire to make each life you touch better.

Day 1

Read: Desire, Associate Scripture Verses and Opening Personal Reflection

Activity: Are you ready? When everything you have waited for begins to come together, it seems nothing can stop us. It's that moment when the switch flips and you put everything you have into your actions. Describe at least two occurrences in your life when desire was at full tilt. (Remember, desire is not always good, but don't worry about that for today's exercise.)

Desire #1

_____

_____

_____

_____

Desire #2

_____

_____

_____

_____

Prayer: Dear Lord, protect me as I face desire along your path. Allow me to use this emotion in the most positive of ways. Use my desire to spread action through your followers. Guide me away from the unproductive things that may enter my mind. In the name of Jesus Christ, I pray. Amen

Day 2

Read: 1 Chronicles 29

Review: Desire notes from Day 1

Activity: Here we begin to see just how much God desires for us to love him. As our relationship with Christ becomes more real and passionate, we are given opportunities in life. God wants us in his life. How much desire for a relationship with him do you show by your actions?

Desire Action

_____

_____

_____

_____

Prayer: Dear Lord, spark that internal flame of mine, so that it may burn strong throughout my life. Allow the results of that desire to be contagious for others in your community. Send me forth to do good on your behalf. In the name of Jesus Christ, I pray. Amen

Day 3

Read: Ecclesiastes 12

Review: Desire Action notes from Day 2

Activity: Today we cover how hard life gets as we grow older. The saying "enjoy it now, because when you get older it is tough" does not have to be true. At the same time, we hear that our children are not growing up as faithful as generations before. How do we more effectively implant a desire for a relationship with Christ in the early years?

Start Young

_____

_____

_____

_____

Prayer: Dear Lord, give me awareness and thoughts today, so that I may
            help the young draw closer to you. Secure their hearts now, so
            that their future is given every opportunity possible. Protect them
            from dead-end roads whose entrances are so brightly lit. In the
            name of Jesus Christ, I pray. Amen

Day 4

Read: Isaiah 55

Review: Start Young notes from Day 3

Activity: In Isaiah 55, we see that we have a partner. His name is God.
            Many actions we take start as desires from him. As more people
            realize that God is our coach, the greater his team will be. He
            is waiting for a "Yes." Describe the feeling of knowing that
            God is on the same team; even your coach. As you express this,
            consider that you are talking to someone on the fence regarding
            Christianity.

God's Team

_____

_____

_____

_____

Prayer: Dear Lord, teach me your ways and instill in me the confidence
            to go forward with desire. I thank you for accepting me on your
            team. May my actions please you and create benefit for the greater
            good. In the name of Jesus Christ, I pray. Amen

Day 5

Read: Desire

Reflect: Your notes from each of the exercises this week

Activity: If you are like me, this week has totally fired you up to take action. Make sure the actions you take are for God. Once you do that, GO! Below, list the desired outcomes in your life and then start planning. Finally, never stop living by the fire inside.

Desired Outcomes

_____

_____

_____

_____

Prayer: Dear Lord, give me hope today for the feeling I have inside. May it be fruitful for your pleasure. Take my desire and align it with your purposes. Once complete, there is nothing that can stop us. Thank you. In the name of Jesus Christ, I pray. Amen

Desire—Closing Personal Reflection

Desire is such a passionate word to not only use, but to also reflect upon. Our lives would be so different without it. When I first started dating my wife, I knew she was "the one". I wanted to be with her all the time. Just by the way I felt for her, I knew it must be God's desire as well. Eventually, it was. However, she had experienced a very difficult relationship before we met and clearly had some healing to do. This is an example of why our desires must align correctly with God's timing and plan.

He did allow our relationship to truly blossom when she was ready. Any time sooner and my desire alone would have pushed her away. Live passionately for God and stay in line with his desires.

I have read and written many letters in my lifetime. However, the letter I wrote my wife-to-be after she emotionally cancelled a date, and effectively our relationship, will be forever in my mind. We had only been on a couple of dates and she was clearly not ready for a long-term relationship. I, however, knew she was the one. I told her that when she was ready I would be there, no matter the length of time. Who in their right mind does that after two dates? I am very lucky that the "freak" label was not put on me forever. I simply knew that God's desire was for us to be together. I was there and now patience was all it would take.

Renew

Life is a series of new beginnings and some not so fortunate endings
Each start has a story with enormous impact on one's direction and ultimate destiny
What you do with these beginnings and endings creates who you are
The "who" is only created by yourself and no one person can force you to change
Only you can recreate the "who;"

There are life events that make you think you are the only one on earth
Divorce and death are near equals when they happen and impact the "who" you thought was you
Death is a physical event that takes your loved one to another place—yet leaves you to ask why
Divorce splits your current and past life with questions of "was it me?" and "what could I have done?"
Only you can recreate the "who;"

Forgiveness is easier said than done—deep pain stays around a while and holds down the "who"
Divorce allows you a second chance at love, to find your true soul mate, who completes you
But it takes so much away from you—trust, honesty, sense of self, dignity, and family
Family is the core of "who"—your father, mother, brother, sister, daughter, and extended family
Only you can recreate the "who;"

How do you focus the "who" again after such events in life occur—look for guidance inside
Pick the target you want to align your life with and never sway from the goal
Allow your target to have spiritual, physical, and mental achievements that let the real "who" out
Recreate the "who" if it has left you because of deep pain and misdirection
Only you can recreate the "who;"

Be sure you line up straight with the target; if you don't, even the best intentions will sway
Allow personal spirituality and drive to keep you on that line
Force learning from previous hurt via death and divorce to create strength and not pity
Do not look back at things you did wrong or regret, but hold tight the target and its happiness
Only you can recreate the "who;"

Finally, you must follow through with the steps you have put in place to achieve your target
If you fall and break your stride, remember, life is full of bumps and learn from them, but continue
There is green grass on the other side of pain and confusion—open up and see what is hiding
Don't let unspeakable acts by others pick the target for "who"—share your greatness with all
Only you can recreate the "who."

It's never too late to pick a target—line up—and follow through.

Associated Scripture Verses

Psalm 51:10
Create in me a pure heart, O God, and renew a steadfast spirit within me.

Isaiah 40:31
... but those who hope in the Lord will renew their strength. They will soar on wings like eagles; they will run and not grow weary, they will walk and not be faint.

2 Corinthians 4:16
Therefore we do not lose heart. Though outwardly we are wasting away, yet inwardly we are being renewed day by day.

Renew—Opening Personal Reflection

There are times in life when we feel like we are on this vast planet all by ourselves. Let me assure you that you are not alone with that feeling. I have been there. If you open your eyes wide enough, you will see us all. We become blinded by our own pain. Actions that you have taken, or others have taken which affected you, can strip all the happiness that years built. When things happen back to back to back, the fall is more difficult and the climb back up seems impossible. The climb is where your strength comes from, because you are climbing with Christ. You are never alone and only you can take the appropriate step forward. If you are down and broken, start to recreate the "who" within you today. I did—so can you!

Day 1

Read: Renew, Associated Scripture Verses and Opening Personal Reflection

Activity: There will be times in your life that will shake you up pretty well. You may already have experienced some. If not, unfortunately, they are coming. But here is the bottom line: Do not let yourself make it worse than it has to be. Unfortunately, I made it rough for myself. Describe below how Renew makes you feel.

Renew Thoughts

_____

_____

_____

_____

Prayer: Dear Lord, allow me to take recommendations from those that
            have come before me. Let these experiences guide my responses to
            the things that will happen in my life. Your healing presence is so
            comforting. Allow me to feel its great soothing as my heart heals.
            In the name of Jesus Christ, I pray. Amen

Day 2

Read: Psalm 51

Review: Renew notes from Day 1

Activity: God shows us that he will forgive any sin as long as we turn to
            him and live for his purposes. Holding grudges for things that
            have happened will only make things worse for you. Describe a
            situation where you harbored ill will against someone, or a group,
            and how it affected you.

Pain Within

_____

_____

_____

_____

Prayer: Dear Lord, allow me to let go of my past pain and suffering. Give me the strength to forgive, as I will never move forward without that action. Show me the way. Few see how great the feeling can be after forgiving. Let me feel this offering. In the name of Jesus Christ, I pray. Amen

Day 3

Read: Isaiah 40

Review: Pain Within notes from Day 2

Activity: This chapter of Isaiah truly shows how hope and renewal are linked to God. When we are nearly at "Rock Bottom", there is really only one place to go: God's word. If we are aligned with him, our falls may not be as hard. Hard is also a personal level. It is determined by how deep you have fallen in the past. How far do you have to fall? Are you connected closely enough to God so as to soften the fall?

Falling with God

_____

_____

_____

_____

Prayer: Dear Lord, accept me more each day, as I continue to work on our relationship in order to spread your word. Your protection is requested to soften the blows in my life, but make sure I learn a lesson from each problem I encounter. In the name of Jesus Christ, I pray. Amen

Day 4

Read: 2 Corinthians 4

Review: Falling with God notes from Day 3

Activity: 2 Corinthians 4:16 is one of my favorite Bible verses. The
accompanying aspects of this chapter are so supportive to this
verse. Take verse 16 and layer in the other aspects from this
chapter to describe what you hear from God.

Hearing from God

_____

_____

_____

_____

Prayer: Dear Lord, your willingness to respond to those in need is
amazing. How often we take for granted the sacrifices you have
made for our benefit and only look to ourselves. Leave in me
an open heart, one that sees the pain and asks for help. Don't
allow me to focus externally, only internally. In the name of Jesus
Christ, I pray. Amen

Day 5

Read: Purpose

Reflect: Your notes from each of the exercises this week

Activity: Have you picked your target this week? Spend the remainder of
your time today working through how you will line up and follow
through with that target.

Target

_____

_____

_____

_____

Prayer: Dear Lord, give me guidance to ensure I am focused on you.
Allow me to take the appropriate actions in my journey and learn
from each step of the way. Show me you are the target. We may
get there separately, but we will all get there. In the name of Jesus
Christ, I pray. Amen

Renew—Closing Personal Reflection

First of all, you should know this is the writing that started it all. The
original title was, "The Who", which I later changed to fit more closely with the
structure of this devotional series. The reason I know God was renewing me is
because this was written in about ten minutes and I never did change even one
word. No revisions, no misspellings—not a thing. Think how I must have felt
when this happened. I had never written anything before.

It became very clear to me that God had written all of this on my heart. I
was simply putting it on paper for the first time. I think that is why 2 Cor. 4:16
is so special to me. Outwardly, I had not healed from my pains felt from the
prior years. However, God has been healing my heart all along the way. Once I
was ready, I saw it. Wow, what a change it made for me. If you are dealing with
something inside, but don't think it will ever get better, ask God for help. He is
always there. Don't try to go it alone—ask for help when you need it.

Finally, there is a concern that someone had for me. Yet I never knew about
it, until he had left to be with God. I was going through a lot of struggles at that
point in my life. I want to answer that concern now, even though it is years later.

"Dad, I am doing great!! It took a while, but I was never alone. You have
always guided me with your servant heart. I miss you terribly. Tell Danny, we

said hello. His daughter has completed my life. Tell him thank you. Mom is doing well. She misses you too!! I look forward to our reunion at Christ's table in his time. I love you. Don't worry. God is here with me too!!"

Silence

The air so still, the leaves seem attached to the grass out front
Daytime noise has yielded only to nature's comforting music
Two of us sit in perfect harmony preparing for what is to come
Fear overcomes me, like a nightmare, upon realizing the silence;

Regrets from years ago will not allow me to enter this place
Comfort is found in continuous motion; yet fulfillment is out of reach
In quiet times, we hear him more clearly—that's not the scary part
The expectation of words from our mouth keeps us away from silence;

Great things grow without a sound, like a flower in the spring
Problems still fester when resolution never reaches audible output
A place so feared, that truly has the greatest of opportunities
Life changing decisions and speed bumps from the past still in silence;

Courage is all that is necessary to breach the fear
Problems find their home on the other side of this step
A true greener pasture is now in sight, as quiet as a baby sleeping
Take the step so feared and join our Father in silence;

Now say the words you have prepared so many times, yet skipped
Reach out for the relationship that changes the world for all
Consider that a moment in silence starts the eternal conversation
Let yourself go, so many have been waiting, break through the silence.

Associated Scripture Verses

Psalm 101:8
Every morning I will put to silence all the wicked in the land; I will cut off every evildoer from the city of the Lord.

1 Peter 2:15
For it is God's will that by doing good you should silence the ignorant talk of foolish men.

Job 29:21
Men listened to me expectantly, waiting in silence for my counsel.

Silence—Opening Personal Reflection

For a lot of people, the most fearful time of any day is silent time. This is the time when all the things we have not done come knocking, the bad things resurface, or maybe worry begins. Silence—God's great equalizer. If you know how to use it, then it can be the most powerful time ever. For those of us that don't mind silence, try not saying anything at lunch with someone who fears silence. You can find out just about anything you want to know—ask my wife. Seriously, spending time in silence gives us time to collect our thoughts, evaluate our relationships and spend quality time with Christ. Don't be afraid of silence. It may bring you answers to questions you have been impatient about in the past.

Day 1

Read: Silence, Associated Scripture Verses and Opening Personal Reflection

Activity: In life we have many regrets and struggles. If we do not handle the healing of those properly, they can continue to pain us for years to come. They affect our time of silence with God because all the bad things surface and it makes us want to run from this time with him. We will fill the silence with just about anything. How does silence affect you in your life?

Silence Impact

_____

_____

_____

_____

Prayer: Dear Lord, (be silent for at least 30 seconds) thank you for the opportunity to hear your words and for you to hear my thoughts. Protect me from harm and show me the way to embrace silence. In the name of Jesus Christ, I pray. Amen

Day 2

Read: Psalm 101

Review: Silence Impact notes from Day 1

Activity: As you read through this Psalm, we continue to see the theme of putting things to silence, most of them evil or wicked. Are there areas in your life that you run from? Spend time thinking about those areas and come up with how you could quiet them forever.

Quiet Topics

_____

_____

_____

_____

Prayer: Dear Lord, show me the way to a silent heart that is full of life and not wickedness. Allow times of silence to create a greater bond between you and me. Thank you for your patience with me. In the name of Jesus Christ, I pray. Amen

Day 3

Read: 1 Peter 2

Review: Quiet Topic notes from Day 2

Activity: When people are against you for whatever reason, do not attack them with words. Focus your attention on the good deeds you have planned. Through God, their words will be silenced. Write down an example or two from your life similar to this, where you either responded with words or deeds. How did it go?

Life Situation #1

_____

_____

_____

_____

Life Situation #2

_____

_____

_____

_____

Prayer: Dear Lord, show me how to take the high road in life. Develop in me the ability to walk away and take action, rather than fight a meaningless fight. However, support me when it is time to stand firm. In the name of Jesus Christ, I pray. Amen

Day 4

Read: Job 29

Review: Life Situation notes from Day 3

Activity: Job looks over his life and reflects on the days when he was in God's favor. Many times people fell silent when he spoke to them. This example is a very simple view of how silence has been used in learning. The people wanted to make sure they heard everything. How much time do you spend in silence each day? Take time today (10 minutes) to just sit in silence, with no phones, computers, TV, anything—just silence. Describe how that felt.

Silent Time

_____

_____

_____

_____

Prayer: Dear Lord, support my objectives with silence in my life. Begin to open my heart to the ideas you have planted there. Take away fear and replace with willingness. Show me the comfort found in silence and help block the fears that make me run from you. In the name of Jesus Christ, I pray. Amen

Day 5

Read: Silence

Reflect: Your notes from each of the exercises this week

Activity: We have three more weeks remaining in this devotional series. Each day, after the provided prayer, add 3-5 minutes of silent prayer before you close. Come back to this page and reflect on how that changed your perspective of silence over the three weeks.

Change in Silence

_____

_____

_____

_____

Prayer: Dear Lord, offer me peace and understanding for new ways to experience your grace. Create conviction during my silent time and prepare my body for the days to come. (3-5 minutes of silence) In the name of Jesus Christ, I pray. Amen

Silence—Closing Personal Reflection

I am one of the few people that absolutely love silence. I can drive from Arkansas to North Carolina and never once turn on the radio. Not really that impressive to many, but our lives are so busy and quiet time is a true gift. We have the opportunity to reflect on our lives, make plans for the future, or just relax. Most people will fill that time with almost anything except silence.

I have heard this said in many different ways: In a situation where a business deal is being made (house, car, etc.) the first person to break the silence will lose. With God, it's not about winners and losers, but it does show that the benefits of silence are real and have an advantage.

Present

One sits with great anticipation of what that box contains
So many items on our list, and each is more important than the other
Moments away from the acceptance of this item and pure excitement
Life suddenly slows to a crawl as a breeze flutters the bow on the present;

Confusion is now staring me in the face like a dog waiting for a treat
The desires held for that box are now in profound conflict
Everything had changed the moment that breeze entered the room
Nothing dramatically; yet, the content now feels very different in my present;

My excitement begins to return as opening this wrapping is near again
All is different on this side of that life changing moment
The list I have is no longer mine, but one that many folks carry
Finally, the time has come to view the contents of this present;

"You are here with me" is written on a note at the bottom of this box
My stillness is only exceeded by the fear in my heart
All expectations drop to the floor and a new understanding is laid at my feet
God has shown me the greatest gift of life; He only wants me to be present;

A request so small that it only takes seconds, but literally changes lives
The cost of this effort has no monetary commitment, but sets us free
Life throws many challenges at each of us throughout our time on Earth
Accept God's gifts and purposes for your life by simply being present.

Associated Scripture Verses

Genesis 33:11
"Please accept the present that was brought to you, for God has been gracious to me and I have all I need. And because Jacob insisted, Esau accepted it.

2 Chronicles 29:29
When the offerings were finished, the king and everyone present with him knelt down and worshipped.

Psalm 14:5
There they are, overwhelmed with dread, for God is present in the company of the righteous.

Present—Opening Personal Reflection

The next time you are at work or at home having a conversation with some-one, ask yourself how much attention you are paying to them and how much is being paid to the next thing on the agenda. I was very surprised at the difficulty of truly being "present," meaning completely in tune while in conversation with others. We juggle so many things in our lives, in the end causing us to not give 100% to anything.

Our decisions are typically based on what we know and hear. If we are so distracted, can you imagine the impact on our decisions? Give the greatest present of all—"presence." Spend real time with God and your family. Close down all the other activities going on in your life for a few hours each day and give quality time to those you love. You will not regret it and they will never forget it.

Day 1

Read: Present, Associated Scripture Verses and Opening Personal Reflection.

Activity: In this writing you will find two separate meanings for the word "present." Describe both below and how they reflect God as a person.

Present #1

_____

_____

_____

_____

Present #2

_____

_____

_____

_____

Prayer: Dear Lord, thank you for the presents you offer to me in my walk
with you. Your gifts are truly a blessing. Allow me to use them to
the best of my abilities. Never let me take for granted that which
you have given me. (3-5 minutes of silence) In the name of Jesus
Christ, I pray. Amen

Day 2

Read: Genesis 33

Review: Present notes from Day 1

Activity: In this chapter Jacob comes back to Esau for the first time
in many years. Jacob is concerned about the reception he
will receive, so he sends a present to Esau. The definition for
"present" here is a gift. Describe how a present can do what
words sometimes can't.

Impact of Presents

_____

_____

_____

_____

Prayer: Dear Lord, give me the understanding that we are all very
different and we receive love in different ways. For those whose
love language is presents, shower them with many gifts. Allow us
all to grow in the special ways that show us thanks. (3-5 minutes
of silence) In the name of Jesus Christ, I pray. Amen

Day 3

Read: 2 Chronicles 29

Review: Impact of Presents notes from Day 2

Activity: We are now introduced to the second definition of "present."
Here it is defined as being with someone. Being present simply
means being there. We can take this to another level by saying we
need to not only be there, but be attentive. Today, I want you to
notice how many things are going on in your head when talking to
others. Stop and listen—be present. Describe how this played out
in your day.

Impact of Present

_____

_____

_____

_____

Prayer: Dear Lord, clear my mind so that I am present to those around me. Show me the difference in life as I become more conscious of the impact I can make on others by making this simple change. (3-5 minutes of silence) In the name of Jesus Christ, I pray. Amen

Day 4

Read: Psalm 14

Review: Impact of Present notes from Day 3

Activity: One thing we can always count on is that God is present and accounted for when we need him. He is always there. This does not mean we get an answer to all our questions immediately, but he is always at work in our lives. How does knowing this impact how you approach God?

Approach to God

_____

_____

_____

_____

Prayer: Dear Lord, continue to be with me as I grow as a person and in my faith. Challenge me to be more present in the lives of the people that are closest to me. Also speak guidance to me, as I am more present in my faith. (3-5 minutes of silence) In the name of Jesus Christ, I pray. Amen

Day 5

Read: Present

Reflect: Your notes from each of the exercises this week.

Activity: Set aside time in your schedule to be with those you truly love. Leave your phone and email alone during this period. Just simply be there with them and let God determine how you spend that time. We all live with regrets at some point; don't let not spending time with your loved ones be one of those regrets. List three people that you need to be present with this week.

People to be present with ...

Person #1

_____

_____

_____

_____

Person #2

_____

_____

_____

_____

Person #3

_____

_____

_____

_____

Prayer: Dear Lord, slow the pace of my life, so that I may prioritize the important things. Ensure that I protect my family time regardless of the pressure from external forces. These are the times I will cherish forever and that will have the greatest impact on me. (3-5 minutes of silence) In the name of Jesus Christ, I pray. Amen

Present—Closing Personal Reflection

With all the electronic devices and geographic separation we have with our families and loved ones, we must make the effort to spend quality time together. That truly is the greatest gift. I certainly remember those times in my past. My father spent a lot of time in and out of hospitals because of his kidney transplant. However, some of my greatest memories are times from the hospital.

I remember one day, the doctors were trying to keep his feet straight up because of blood flow concerns. There were many options on how to keep his feet that way, but one was priceless. You would have to know my dad. He was very conservative and given his illness, he really could not do many sports, so his shoe collection was pretty straightforward. Work shoes, beating around the house shoes, church shoes and working in the yard shoes were pretty much it.

Well, the doctor told us one of the options was to wear high top basketball shoes. That option was taken immediately. We bought these huge shoes and put them on him. It was hilarious to see him in a hospital bed with cords and monitors all over and these brand new high-tops sticking out of the sheets at the end of the bed. Something I will truly never forget and I smile each time I think of that day.

Just be present, you never know when a moment like that will occur in your life. Be ready.

Confusion

She brings out a new feeling of compassion you have missed
Can you be sure that it is not misguided by opportunity?
You want it to be permanent, yet rushing it is not right
My heart wants so badly for it to be, but fear settles in;

The days are full of "what ifs" and followed by thoughts of "how does she feel?"
The answer you want to hear is equally as interested
Why can't you ask the question and accept the answer?
Complete dedication is on the tip of your tongue, yet so hard to execute;

Am I scared of what might be a little too early, too soon?
If your feelings provide you a sense of security, they can't be wrong—right?
But what if you get the opposite of your wish and rejection happens?
Can you not risk, what your heart tells you is right?

She makes my days seem like I am a complete person again
I wake with a bright gleam of opportunity and new experiences
I close the day looking forward to what might be next, reflecting on excitement
Yet, I can't take the reins and ask for her feelings for me;

Her beauty is so internally deep that external beauty is but a glimmer
Yet gives me chills to consider her sight a part of my every day
There is so much right and so much I don't know and want to realize
She makes me think of nothing but pleasure and a peaceful existence;

Can I wait and just let God's path be developed for me?
Do I insert my desires into her stream of thought to get reflection?
Is she ready for me to provide all the built-up emotions ready to explode?
I want to ... I know it is right ... the words come from my heart and stop short;

You can never have what you are not willing to realize
I could stop now and let my life take its course—but miss time
The thought of this day has driven your every moment forward
Take the initiative and let what is your desire breathe; yet again fear;

Could you be wrong, and it is just a new emotion or new blade of life?
What if that darkness that has been growing for years, now only sees sunshine for growth?
Life is a short existence with decisions that plague your progress forward
She completes your journey, but might it be too early to expand—follow your heart.

Why not see?

Associated Scripture Verses

1 Samuel 14:20
Then Saul and all his men assembled and went to the battle. They found the Philistines in total confusion, striking each other with their swords.

Acts 19:32
The assembly was in confusion: Some were shouting one thing, some another. Most of the people did not even know why they were there.

Galatians 5:10
I am confident in the Lord that you will take no other view. The one who is throwing you into confusion will pay the penalty, whoever he may be.

Confusion – Opening Personal Reflection

Welcome to the one place we have all visited—Confusion Central—at the intersection of "Here we go" and "No way I am going there." On one side, we are so ready to jump into whatever it may be. Yet right before we move, concrete sets in and nothing happens. Knowing what to do is hard sometimes, but if we take the time to think through our issues and lay out the pros and cons, it can be much simpler. Ask God for guidance and try to understand what the impact of a few more days, weeks or even years might be. Sometimes our confusion is caught between what we want and what we know is right. This one is tough, but usually bet on the "what is right" to put you in God's grace. Sometime all it takes is time to clear your mind.

Day 1

Read: Confusion, Associated Scripture Verses and Opening Personal Reflection

Activity: As much as we would like for life to be very cut and dry, it is anything but that. When you think everything is clear, boom, something happens out of left field. I finally realized that is life and I must embrace it and learn along the way. How do you handle life's confusing moments?

Confusing Moment

_____

_____

_____

_____

Prayer: Dear Lord, show me the way. Give me direction in my times of absolute confusion. Ensure that I stay grounded when challenged and ready when prompted. Provide me with clarity of the mind necessary to let your time be my watch, given that you have orchestrated the events in my life. (3-5 minutes of silence) In the name of Jesus Christ, I pray. Amen.

Day 2

Read: 1 Samuel 14

Review: Confusing Moment notes from Day 1

Activity: Confusion can cause us to make bad judgment calls, whether small or large. In this case the Philistines were killing each other, acting completely out of their minds. Later we find Jonathan tasting honey when he was told not to. Has success confused his mind as to who really is in control? Describe a decision made during a confusing period for you that caused a problem in your life.

Confused Decision

_____

_____

_____

_____

Prayer: Dear Lord, offer me clarity of mind as I travel through life's choices. Lead me in making the right decisions. Protect others that are affected by my decisions. Provide me comfort when hard decisions affect others only because you are leading them in a new direction. (3-5 minutes of silence) In the name of Jesus Christ, I pray. Amen

Day 3

Read: Acts 19

Review: Your notes from Day 2

Activity: Confusion sinks in when we don't understand why something has happened. This assumes that we were supposed to know why. Do you think that confusion in our mortal life can be linked all the way back to the tree of knowledge and life in the Garden of Eden? Did original sin cause this pain that we are still experiencing?

Confusion Root Cause

_____

_____

_____

_____

Prayer: Dear Lord, give me knowledge of only that which you desire me to know. Supply me with a mind of trust, so that I don't desire more than I should. Provide me clarity at your appropriate moments. Let others see in you what I see and may they grow rapidly in faith. (3-5 minutes of silence) In the name of Jesus Christ, I pray. Amen.

Day 4

Read: Galatians 5

Review: Your notes from Day 3

Activity: In this chapter of Galatians, we see that freedom comes through Christ. So why do we have to give up so many things in order to be with him? Describe below how a non-believer can be easily confused by having to give up him- or herself and follow these guidelines to be connected with Christ.

Giving to Get

_____

_____

_____

_____

Prayer: Dear Lord, open my mind to simplify my decisions as I work through a confused world. I realize how great walking with you is; yet others are confused by "why." Help me to spread your word more effectively, so that many more can see what I have seen. (3-5 minutes of silence) In the name of Jesus Christ, I pray. Amen.

Day 5

Read: Confusion

Reflect: Your notes from each of the exercises this week.

Activity: Up to this point, we have left Satan out of our discussion. We know he is always sitting around and waiting for a moment of weakness or confusion. Confusion seems like the topic of choice for him. How do you think Satan plays a role in God's purposes as it relates to confusion?

Satan and Confusion

_____

_____

_____

_____

Prayer: Dear Lord, guide me as I allow myself to see the pain that Satan brings in the form of confusion. Give me the pillars of strength to hold up your glory when internally challenged. Cast out his presence in my life so that you may be clearer. (3-5 minutes of silence) In the name of Jesus Christ, I pray. Amen

Confusion—Closing Personal Reflection

Confusion was written at a very pivotal point in my life. I was trying to trust, after a few painful experiences related to this topic. Many times I was so ready to just lay out everything I was thinking and get some feedback, but I could not do it. I was caught between how great it would be to know how someone felt and the "what if they really do not care?" The real question was: Am I ready to hear the answer regardless? And the truth was: "No!"

Sometimes we get confused and impatient, because we want to take action. However, we are nowhere near ready for the response we may receive. Be patient. Take your time and ask God for guidance all along the way. Finally, never create confusion for own gain. I would rather be confused 100% of the time, than ever plant confusion in someone else for personal gain. You would not only be walking, but probably running from God at that point. Help others. Don't make it harder for them. Stay focused; life is not easy.

Hope

The chase begins when life's challenges turn the wrong way
Structures in our world do not seem as strong now
Seizing the moment is all you have, because tomorrow is not guaranteed
Forward thinking is only a dream without options providing hope;

Alone at heaven's intersection with our Maker is where we find ourselves
Our emotions are at light speed, knowing the decision to be made
Your past gloom is real, yet at this moment the light of life is there
Asking for forgiveness of your sins will open the door of hope;

On the other side, life blossoms like the colors of a rainbow
Days seem like they last longer and nights don't seem as scary
Tomorrow and our future now seem a reality, full of obtainable dreams
All has changed because of this request. All I have now is hope;

Your time did not come to spend eternity with your Maker
By letting your sins be forgiven by God, your future changed
Amazement was what you experienced when the meeting was over
The legacy left behind is still challenged because it was your last hope;

Now you meet God at the crossroads of life, and all is bright
The focus of your life is clear in God's eyes, so peaceful in acceptance
Your legacy was written before you took your last breath on earth
Gone from the physical, but triumphant in everlasting hope.

Make hope a reality, not a dream

Associated Scripture Verses

Job 11:18
You will be secure, because there is hope; you will look about you and take your rest in safety.

Psalm 25:5
. . . guide me in your truth and teach me, for you are God my Savior, and my hope is in you all day long.

Psalm 33:20
We wait in hope for the Lord; he is our help and our shield.

Hope—Opening Personal Reflection

The last place anyone wants to spend time is in a hopeless society. Life has thrown me many curve balls over the last decade, but one thing that I have not lost is hope. Having faith in God is essential to having hope. Christ is always the lantern in our darkest days. As ships sail across the Atlantic to North America, the one constant thing is the lighthouse. This light provides all the hope necessary for tired sailors to know the end is within sight. Never give up hope. At times, that is all we have. Hope for a better afternoon, a better tomorrow, a better you, a new medicine, or a new person in your life. Finally, but most importantly, a hope of acceptance into God's kingdom.

Day 1

Read: Hope, Associated Scripture Verses and Opening Personal Reflection

Activity: Hope is the greatest thing any one of us can have. Regardless of the scenarios we find ourselves in, we should never give up hope. Describe a time in your life or that of someone you know where the only thing to cling to was hope. What was it like?

Hope Stretch

_____

_____

_____

_____

Prayer: Dear Lord, offer me assistance when I hold up the hand of hope. Reach for me when I am in my time of need. Give me guidance when those around me hold on to that last hope. Provide them with a sign of better days. (3-5 minutes of silence) In the name of Jesus Christ, I pray. Amen.

Day 2

Read: Job 11

Review: Hope Stretch notes from Day 1

Activity: When God is with us, there is always hope. However, it seems that some people run from God because they feel the situation they are in exists because God did not protect them. They find difficulty going back to him and simply asking for help. How would you explain this situation to someone who is running from God? What are the keys to understanding that God is only one U-turn away?

Hope Turn

_____

_____

_____

_____

Prayer: Dear Lord, please do not let my pride get in the way of our relationship. Continue to stay with me and show me signs of your grace, so that I can make the turn more easily. Give me a heart of strength to make all obstacles in my life be removed by the power of hope. (3-5 minutes of silence) In the name of Jesus Christ, I pray. Amen.

Day 3

Read: Psalm 25

Review: Hope Turn notes from Day 2

Activity: David speaks to the Lord throughout this Psalm, asking for forgiveness of sin and protection from the evildoers. We are asked to follow the covenants laid out in the Old Testament and then God will give us hope in all we do. Describe how success or perception of success by those not following God's word affects hope.

Hope Impact

_____

_____

_____

_____

Prayer: Dear Lord, show me how a life dedicated to you will culminate with all the hope I need. Continue to allow my faith to strengthen, even though I see others benefit from short-term success. Let me fight the fight for hope; not only for me, but for all those around me. (3-5 minutes of silence) In the name of Jesus Christ, I pray. Amen.

Day 4

Read: Psalm 33

Review: Hope Impact notes from Day 3

Activity: In Psalm 33, we again see that only the purposes from God will prevail. Life with God does not come very easy if we continue to look to self for direction. Yet our only hope is for God's grace to protect us and guide us along. Describe how hope is revealed to you in this Psalm.

Hope Revealed

_____

_____

_____

_____

Prayer: Dear Lord, grant us the hope that brightens futures and changes lives. Show us how to turn to you when the battle inside begins. Please protect us from ourselves as we move through life. (3-5 minutes of silence) In the name of Jesus Christ, I pray. Amen.

Day 5

Read: Hope

Reflect: Your notes from each of the exercises this week.

Activity: Take time to think about your greatest hope from God. We all have ideas in our hearts and minds for how God can use us to better his kingdom. Ask God for the hope you have inside. Use the space below to formally make that request.

Hope Request

_____

_____

_____

_____

Prayer: Dear Lord, grant me time to focus more intently on your wishes for me. Show me that regardless of what I may have done or where I have come from; your arms of hope are always there. Please remind me of that during times of challenge. (3-5 minutes of silence). In the name of Jesus Christ, I pray. Amen.

Hope—Closing Personal Reflection

There is an acronym for hope that I like to use : Humble Option Pointing to Eternity. God provides us eternal life through him; we should take the time necessary to line up with that opportunity. I feel that the word hope gives brightness to every situation. There were truly times when hope was all I had. If you have been there, then you understand completely. For those that have not experienced the "hands of hope;" my wish for you is that you walk closely with God, so that the request is easily provided when needed. Either way, never, ever give up hope for yourself or hope that someone will turn from a negative lifestyle. You may be that hope for them. Don't stop— God never does.

It is my hope that when you hear this word used by others in your life, it will spark attention and encourage you to help in any way possible. Make sure you lift your hopes to God and ask others to do the same. The phrase, "I have given up hope for ..." is the most tragic of all things spoken. God is always with us and never does he run out of hope. Just run to him. He will be waiting with his "hands of hope" to catch you.

The Core Meaning—Closing Personal Reflection

I would like to start by saying thank you for selecting this book for your devotional time. I certainly hope that you have enjoyed each section and gained a stronger relationship with Christ along the way. Just simply writing this book took my spiritual life to new heights. Life seems to be much simpler when we focus on the aspects of life that truly matter and stay connected to Christ's word each and every day. One thing that I am continually reminded of is that our journey with Christ will never exist without stumbles along the path. But if we stay connected with him frequently, the peaks are higher and the valleys are not as painful.

My first passion is my family. Remember, the initial spark for me was the fear of not having the answers my daughter might seek about Christianity. I have been blessed with great people to spend my time with each day. My wife and daughter are my rocks. Ensure that you and your family spend time with Christ together. The youth of today are very important in the continued spreading of God's word. There are many distractions in life and materialistic desires get in the way. Don't forget that most important relationship—yours with Christ. A spiritually grounded family can start with the parents and spread to the children. However, if your parents are struggling with their faith, don't wait for them to offer Christ. Offer them hope through your faith. It is never too late to turn to God. He already knows our sin, so don't worry. You have been forgiven.

My second passion is to help other people. I prefer to help in a servant leader way, which to me is helping without recognition. When someone in need gets help without knowing it was from you—that is so rewarding. By approaching each other in this manner, we do not get caught up in the responsive help cycle. I refer to that as a "now I have to do something for them" mode. That cycle can get out of hand quickly. Help people just to help, don't expect anything in return. As an example, ten percent of all sales proceeds from this book will go directly to the Sonrise School in Rwanda. Let me make sure you understand that I don't tell you this for the credit of doing something good. The children of that school may never see me, but I will know they are getting a better chance. Even if I visit (which I plan to do) I do not want to be thanked for what I have done. It will be clear on the faces of each and every child.

Finally, please visit my website (www.thecoremeaning.com). There you will find additional information about this book, my journey and links to some of my favorite books. The books you find there, have inspired me along the way. I hope that you will enjoy them. I also encourage you to give your feedback. I would really appreciate your thoughts (positive or negative) about this devotional. In addition, if you or a group you may be part of would like to have me come and discuss the book in more detail, you will find out how to contact me on the website. I hope to see you again in the 2nd book of this series.

May God bless you in everything you do!!

Scripture Index

Old Testament

New Testament

Book	Verse	Page #	Devotional
Matthew	5:4	74	Comfort
Acts	2:17	28	Dreams
Acts	7:22	44	Action
Acts	17:26	66	Determination
Acts	19:32	116	Confusion
Romans	6:23	60	Gift
Romans	8:28	8	Purpose
Romans	12:2	18	Transform
1 Corinthians	12:11	66	Determination
2 Corinthians	3:18	18	Transform
2 Corinthians	4:16	94	Renew
2 Corinthians	5:5	8	Purpose
2 Corinthians	9:2	44	Action
Galatians	5:10	116	Confusion
Philippians	3:21	18	Transform
1 Timothy	1:16	36	Patience
2 Timothy	1:9	8	Purpose
Hebrews	6:12	36	Patience
James	1:17	60	Gift
James	2:17	44	Action
1 Peter	2:15	102	Silence
Revelations	22:17	60	Gift

Made in the USA
Charleston, SC
01 June 2011